HOW TO INCREASE EXECUTIVE EFFECTIVENESS

How to Increase Executive Effectiveness

EDITED BY
EDWARD C. BURSK
EDITOR OF THE *Harvard Business Review* AND
MEMBER OF THE FACULTY, HARVARD GRADUATE
SCHOOL OF BUSINESS ADMINISTRATION

CAMBRIDGE, MASSACHUSETTS
HARVARD UNIVERSITY PRESS
1955

FOURTH PRINTING

Distributed in Great Britain by
GEOFFREY CUMBERLEGE
OXFORD UNIVERSITY PRESS
LONDON

Library of Congress Catalog Card Number 53-12522
Printed in the United States of America

PREFACE

This book, the sixth in an annual series published by the Harvard University Press, is based on the proceedings of the Twenty-Third National Business Conference, sponsored by the Harvard Business School Association, June 13, 1953, which was attended by some 1,400 businessmen — alumni and friends of the School — from all over the country and abroad.

The general theme of the Conference was "How to Increase Executive Effectiveness." The morning session, consisting of four speeches developing the major company policies needed for this purpose, is covered in Part I. The afternoon session, consisting of six panels dealing with specific areas of management, is covered in Part II.

The afternoon panels were conducted purposely on a very informal basis, in an attempt to let the subject develop as the group desired. Short talks by the panel members, aimed primarily at providing factual material from their own experience and establishing their individual positions within the general subject area, were followed by a question and answer period. As happened at previous Conferences, the discussion which ensued was dynamic and spontaneous; and all together it took up the major portion of the afternoon. As far as possible, this material has been reorganized into an orderly, consistent form, and fitted into the chapter-sections representing the observations of the various panel members.

Needless to say, the views expressed in any chapter or chapter-section are the responsibility of the individual author identified in the note at the beginning of the chapter, and as such are not necessarily representative of other authors or the Harvard Business School Association.

I want to thank Miss Louise B. Morse and Miss Virginia B. Fales for their very able editorial assistance.

Edward C. Bursk

I wish to thank [illegible] and Miss Virginia B. Ellis [illegible] of the manuscript.

[illegible] Edward C. Bursk

CONTENTS

PART I

PART II

SUPPLEMENT

PART I

INTRODUCTION OF THE THEME

Donald K. David

I am delighted to welcome readers to this book, based on the Twenty-Third National Business Conference at the Harvard Business School. It is the most recent in the series of books based on similar conferences over the past five years.

Each of these conferences has developed a theme. This has usually been some aspect of administration — for example, the "Encouragement of Individual Initiative," "Getting Things Done in Business," "Thinking Ahead for Business." Our development of these subjects has usually centered attention upon both the importance and the responsibilities of executive leadership. A master theme running through the last half dozen meetings has been the professional obligations of which business is growing more conscious. The conference of 1948, for example, was devoted directly to the "*Responsibilities* of Business Leadership." In 1949, the forerunner of this year's subject, "The *Development* of Executive Leadership," was the theme.

Here we shall consider *how* to increase executive effectiveness. Our definition of effectiveness will take into account our developing concepts of professional obligations, our knowledge of business life, and our capacity to look beyond our present jobs and horizons. None of us — authors or readers — will be equipped with pat answers when the end of the book is reached, but various ways of thinking constructively *about* the problem will be available for our choice and use.

NOTE: Mr. David is Dean of the Harvard Graduate School of Business Administration.

My insistence upon professional responsibility should not be misunderstood. As I have said before, I do not believe that business is yet a profession, though it may become one. But whatever the current status of business practice, those who read this book, along with those attending the conference on which it is based, by their very interest commit themselves to professional ideals and aspirations. Professional standards and professional skill in *practicing* administration are equally necessary in today's business world. This is the conviction of the Harvard Business School, and this is the challenge to a full exploration of the theme before us. Executive effectiveness must include success in recognizing and discharging the commitments which today bind the businessman to purposes far more extensive than his immediate self-interest.

Executive effectiveness includes more than the achievement of a profitable record, though this is a primary obligation. It is more than individual brilliance and personal ability to perceive and solve problems. The good executive is an administrator in the broadest sense. And an administrator is effective only when the purposes of a business organization and the essential satisfactions of its individual members are being achieved. The competent administrator is necessarily a builder of organization, a man experienced in achieving coöperation without either bogging down in the swamp of compromise or evading the unpleasant adjustments essential in a competitive society. He works in a web of responsibilities, many of which can be in conflict with one another. Executive effectiveness is in part the ability to strike continual balances among responsibilities to oneself, one's company, associates, industry, and community.

Against the background of so sweeping a definition — and no narrower one will be equal to our needs — it is clear that no one at any moment, no matter how extensive his experience, is effective *enough*. The tasks of self-development in administrative ability and of providing the conditions for the development of others know no final boundaries. Progress requires the better understanding of the technical and human problems of business which can be achieved through education and research related to the administrative process. Individual growth in administrative ability, allied to the support of inquiry into its components, can be a continuing challenge. It can, as much as anything, give meaning and importance to a lifetime in business and provide the permanent satisfactions that financial reward alone cannot equal.

This subject is important for reasons other than the satisfactions which "effectiveness" provides to those who try to develop it to serve professional ends. Within a company managerial competence is important, particularly at the level where the shortage of top-flight ability is most keenly felt. The value of machines and the importance of capital are well recognized. Amounts are attached to them in the balance sheet. Probably the most important asset of a company, however, is its men and women — and, among them, their leaders. No adequate inventory valuation is kept. In too many cases, instead of being the first item of concern in business, the level of administrative effectiveness has not been given conscious attention.

But the scales are coming into balance as managements awake to the importance of continuous growth and its need for day-by-day attention. This is good, for executive ability is needed in many places. Already short in American business, it is needed in local and national government and in business overseas. Here is a quality the world much requires, for the economy of nations and of the free world cannot long proceed without the participation of professional administrators. Perpetuation of a free society depends upon prompt and equitable industrialization of undeveloped countries, upon freer trade, and upon the extension of American productivity to the world in which America has risen to leadership. Leadership is nothing without the men who lead. Those men must know *how* to be continually more effective.

How is the crucial question. None of us has the final answers, but we must consider the question. *How* can we increase our own effectiveness and help others to develop theirs? In the exploration of this question, I invite all readers to join. We would be over-confident if we set out upon this quest with the expectation of achieving a set of rules or infallible guides. But we can advance our thinking by sharing in the ideas, as set forth on the following pages, of men who have themselves made truly professional careers out of their business assignments.

CREATING THE PROPER CLIMATE

Frederick C. Crawford

Today one of America's greatest problems is the development of better management. So strongly do I feel this that I believe our country's very future is tied up with our ability to develop business leadership.

We live in a great industrial age. The outstanding fact of our age is the extraordinary productivity of modern American industry, and I mean industry in the broadest sense — all business, banking, merchandising, manufacturing, and so forth.

Many of us may wish that the American people were more concerned with spiritual and intellectual progress, but today is a material age. People want things. All over the world people want things. The very expressions we use indicate material things — "ill-clad," "ill-housed," "dollar shortage," "standard of living." Dollar shortage simply means wanting things beyond our ability to pay for them.

When we speak of America's power, we mean her ability to produce coal and steel and guns and ships and airplanes. Surely, when history is written, the great increase in the production of wealth will stand out as the prominent fact of our age.

For a thousand years people have dreamed of an abundance and the end of poverty. Today in America that dream is almost realized. But far more astonishing is the possibility of doubling America's productivity in the next ten years. Industry is just on the threshold of great things. At its disposal are extraordinary new methods and controls of production. And the tremendous developments in engi-

NOTE: Mr. Crawford is Chairman of the Board, Thompson Products, Inc.

neering, chemistry, and physics are giving the production man remarkable tools with which to increase productivity.

Here are a few examples:

By eliminating gas furnaces and putting in automatic electric furnaces, forge-shop production is multiplied four times.

The other day at an automobile company, I saw one machine doing the work of 49 men.

In Italy, where coal is mined by hand methods, production averages only 0.4 ton per day per worker. In England this rate is 1⅛ tons. By contrast, the present output rate in America is over 6 tons. Even so, 50 tons of coal per day per worker will soon become a reality at one of our great steel companies, thanks to modern equipment.

In short, given better tools, better management, and the coöperation of labor, we can double our productivity in ten years. Think what this means. Doubling our productivity means halving the cost; and cost determines price. Halving the price means doubling the purchasing power of all.

I believe this increase in productivity is a guarantee of America's freedom. It would solve our economic problems by enabling us to pay our debts, control inflation, raise the standard of living. And it would give us the material strength to prevent war or to win war.

The natural reaction is: "Wonderful! Why don't we get on with it?"

But the matter is not that simple. There is grave danger that this increase in productivity will never be realized. Industry is being attacked from every side. Although people want to share the new wealth and the abundance, they do not understand the basic principles that govern production of wealth. The very increase in wealth tends to increase the pressure to socialize industry and prevent the attainment of higher productivity.

The explanation for this lies partially in the comparative recentness of the great spurt in productivity. Two-thirds of all industrial development has come since I was in college. In my boyhood the atom was believed indivisible; transmission of the human voice by radio was considered impossible; and the airplane was a toy.

American industry has progressed so fast and become so complex that few understand how it functions.

Once upon a time men believed that the world was flat. They did not understand geography — we can call it a sort of geographical illiteracy — and progress was held up for thousands of years. Just so, today, there is widespread *economic* illiteracy. Unless the American people understand this industrial world we live in, they will tax it, regulate it, control it, socialize it, and rob it of existence. That is what is happening in many parts of the world today.

On a recent trip around the world it was my privilege to talk to businessmen. In every country I asked this question: "Why don't you make faster business progress?" And in every country I received this answer: "We can't get going. Too much government, too much socialism, too much bureaucracy, too much regulation, too much taxation."

I believe that America's real danger is 90 per cent an internal one, and lies in the failure to understand how industry operates. The solution, of course, lies in education and understanding and leadership.

And now we are back to our subject: How can we develop business leaders to manage this coming burst of productivity so important to America? How can we develop business statesmen who will be able to interpret and explain the industrial age that we live in?

My assignment is to discuss the "climate" that business must establish to aid in the development of better executives. The major responsibility for creating a proper climate falls upon the top executive. Every institution reflects the personality and character of the boss, whether he likes it or not. What the boss is interested in, the whole organization will be interested in. Thus the boss himself sets the *type* of climate.

There are a few things the top executive must understand when he tackles the proposition of climate.

First, management is made up of human beings. Human beings

are the most interesting things in all of business. As I watch business grow, I become more and more convinced that human relations, public relations, customer relations, and employee relations are all one and the same thing. Why has it taken us 50 years to find this out?

Human emotions are strong motivating forces. We do not turn on will power. It is our emotions that turn on will power. Men do things because of pride, greed, fear, vengeance, hate, self-respect, generosity, integrity, justice, love. Every man can be lazy, antagonistic, harsh, scheming, industrious, coöperative, understanding, loyal. Climate helps determine which of the emotions shall control.

Every man has potentiality for being something of the hero or something of the villain. In my company we have a saying, "The job of management is to get the good out of a man without letting the bad interfere."

Another thing that top management must realize in planning a good climate is that men can no longer be driven. They must be led. The work of the world is done not by geniuses — though they play their part — but by average men, pulling together. And average Americans, pulling together, rise above the average.

It is not easy to get men of unlike viewpoints to work together and respect one another. Nevertheless, modern management needs a team and the viewpoint of every individual member of the team.

In addition, the boss must realize that modern management needs inspiring leadership — a leadership that can be a fountain of enthusiasm, that bubbles best when times go hard. I think Walter Chrysler was just such an inspirational leader. He had the power first to draw men around him and then to draw the very best out of them.

Business is the greatest game in the world — the matching of wits. It beats any poker game. In my company we have learned that "good luck" is not fortunate happenstance, after all. "Good luck" is good preparation; it is careful planning to win on either break.

Another thing the business leader must learn is that a "stuffed shirt" formality has no place in modern management. An atmosphere of informality with a sense of responsibility shared and the door open to all—especially to the younger men—is a key to a successful climate.

A prime essential of the management that can create and foster the right climate is a very high code of personal honor. Watching industry grow for 35 years has convinced me there is but one indispensable rule in business: the Golden Rule.

I have great faith in the goodness of the American worker. The leadership that can build his confidence and morale is the leadership that possesses absolute honesty and integrity of purpose. A worker-manager relationship like this makes an unbeatable team. As one of my own managers said to me: "You can take my money, my machinery, and my buildings. Just leave me my team, and I will have all the business back in two years."

Let us look now at just a few of the simple things that help create climate.

(1) Spot promising young men—the management of the future. In our business we plot "depth" of management agewise. Let me explain. We look through the organization for young men who give promise of management ability, who someday may develop into top executives. Then we make a chart with lines indicating 60, 50, 40, 30, 20 years. On it we plot the ages of these young men. This shows whether we have distribution of management potential in each age bracket.

It is amazing how few names qualify for this chart. Though we employ 25,000 workers, less than 40 men appear on our chart. On them falls a tremendous responsibility because it is from their ranks that tomorrow's top managers must come.

(2) Expose these young men to the problems of the business. Problems are opportunities.

A young man once came to me for a job. When I inquired what he wanted, he said, "An opportunity."

"Do you really know what you mean by 'opportunity'?" I asked. He replied, "Of course, I know what I want. I want an office with my name on the door, a mahogany desk, and a secretary."

"No, you don't," I told him. "Those are only the end items that you may get after you have developed your opportunity. An opportunity is a problem — a problem the boss doesn't know the answer to."

Every modern business has an abundance of unsolved problems. Urge each young man to take one of them and try to solve it.

When I graduated from engineering school, the president of a large steel fabricating company interviewed some of us graduates. When he offered me a job, I was very proud. Just before leaving, I said, "Mr. X, let me ask you one question: If you were in my shoes, would you accept this?"

"No, I would not," he answered. "I would go to a smaller company where there are hundreds of problems not yet solved."

I followed his advice. I joined a small company, poorly organized and plagued with problems. When there was no money, I was a collection agent. When there were no orders, I was a salesman. When production was so disorganized as to be tantamount to none at all, I was a production trouble-shooter.

In 1929 when the crash came and we had no orders and no money and no production, I got the job of manager. I did not realize then what an extraordinary business training I was getting.

(3) Clearly outline the company's objectives and policies to these young men. A management guide is helpful. Frequent management review meetings are important.

General Marshall once told me that the American soldier could be a good or a bad soldier. The difference was this: if you explained to him what the objective was, why and when it should be captured — and it made sense to him — he was the greatest soldier in the world. Just so in training for business management, interpretation and understanding of the objective are important.

(4) Delegate responsibility — always with authority as well as with accountability. The delegation of responsibility is necessary to develop the abilities of a man, but without authority it creates frustration and destroys initiative.

And without accountability, things can run wild. Accountability develops control, judgment, and self-discipline; and it brings the young man back to earth again should he soar too high.

It is not easy to delegate. I know many businesses in which the older men tend to hold on to the reins and draw them closer, thereby creating an increasingly centralized management.

(5) Eliminate fear of criticism—not criticism itself, but fear of criticism. This is very important in creating climate. Fear of criticism can crush vision, can wet-blanket enthusiasm. All men are sensitive, and the most visionary are the most sensitive.

Listen to and encourage all suggestions. Once a young man in our business said he wanted to start an aluminum foundry in order to meet a certain problem. Although his proposal sounded unwise, I did not want to dampen his enthusiasm. So I appropriated the funds necessary to start the foundry, and out of it grew our great aluminum division.

Another young man came to me and said, "I think war is coming. We ought to have a war plant. Let's try to get one." Fantastic as it seemed to me, I said, "All right, then, go to Washington and see what you can do." He came back with a thirty-million-dollar plant. It changed the whole character of our business!

I asked a young manager who had reached the top quickly what single thing helped him most in his rather brilliant career. He thought awhile, then said, "One thing stands out: I could think out loud with my superiors. I could throw out crazy suggestions. I could talk over any subject without fear that I would be squelched. It had more effect upon my development as a manager than anything else."

(6) Urge the young men to make decisions without fear of making mistakes. This again is very important. Mistakes are the very soil of progress. Mistakes are experience. Experience develops judgment. And judgment is necessary to good management.

In 1922 my predecessor said to me, "Our little Michigan plant is a mess. Its losses last year exceeded its sales, and that is something! I'm sending you up there as manager, and here are your instructions: Either kill that plant and bury it, or revive it and make it into something. I don't care what you do, but do something!"

I went to Michigan. I made mistakes. They cost $100,000 the first year, but five years later the little plant had expanded fifteen times, and was on its way up instead of out. This, surely, is a good example of some of the things I've been discussing: a clear statement of objectives, exposure to a problem, delegated responsibility, and encouragement to make decisions, regardless of mistakes. The experience had a profound effect upon my business career.

The president of a steel company said this to me the other day about one of his young men: "That man is very important to this company. We have invested a million dollars in his mistakes. We are going to watch him."

And Edison once said to a discouraged young man, "Yes, you have failed 2,000 times, but what progress that is! Now we know that there are 2,000 ways that won't work."

In my company we have a philosophy that is helpful. Whenever we run into difficulty on a customer's order — as we do from time to time — we say, "Splendid! Here's a chance to show that customer how quickly we can correct this. He'd never have known how good we are if we hadn't got into trouble."

(7) Never criticize in front of others. The right kind of criticism can build a man's confidence, pride, ambition, and loyalty; the wrong kind can destroy them.

(8) Pay well. Have a good pay system that works. Don't make men wonder about their pay. If a man is good and knows he is good, delay in fair pay advancement does not help morale.

(9) Have a sound promotion policy. Here many of my business friends fall down. A sound policy involves readiness to move the older men up into staff positions, and to push young men into operating responsibility where managers are made. It calls for recognition of talent and promotion from within. At the same time, it demands alertness to any need for new blood, and prompt action to avoid inbreeding by bringing in the exceptional outside man.

It is here that you often meet the problem of relatives. Although it need not be a source of trouble, it usually is, and some companies have a rule prohibiting the employment of relatives.

Promotion comes in two ways: in moving a man, when he is ready, to a larger job; and, more often, in backing him up and supplying capital to his division so that he can grow and develop to his full capacity. The latter is often the faster promotion.

(10) Build up deserving men in the eyes not only of the company but of the community as well. A pat on the back is a powerful stimulant. Every young man wants the boss to know what he is doing. Every young man wants to think that the boss thinks it is something important.

Recognition before one's fellows encourages enthusiasm and self-confidence. We are all emotional creatures. We all in greater or less degree have a feeling of inferiority, and recognition is a salutary antidote.

(11) Encourage outside activities. Here many of my business friends are not up to date. Of course, participation in outside affairs takes time, but it pays dividends in the development of management leadership. Responsibility assumed in the community — the church, the hospital, the school, the library, the welfare agency — in trade associations and technical societies, and in government makes for better managers as well as for better citizens. And not to be overlooked is the good will it can earn for the company.

It is here that the importance of public speaking is most clearly demonstrated. The ability to think on one's feet and to talk on one's feet is an absolute requisite of modern management. In my company all division managers must talk every 90 days to the men they work for. I have yet to find a man who could not learn to talk about the things he is trying to do.

To assume leadership in this great industrial nation and explain how it functions is all part of the broad job of developing statesmanship.

(12) Incentive pay exerts a powerful influence in creating climate for executive effectiveness. It seems to me that there are two simple rules of incentive: (a) The value of incentive pay is proportional to the impact on the man. (b) Incentive pay is far more important at the higher levels.

Consider (a). Immediate reward for effort has a profound effect upon a man. We know how effective piecework can be. Group work is less so. I was interested to learn recently that a plant, which was owned by the employees themselves through purchase, voted to strike. Ownership was too remote to have an immediate effective impact upon the workers.

Consider (b). One hundred years ago man-effort was the most important and almost the only element of production. Today there are two more elements in productivity: first, tools; second, methods and controls. One hundred years ago man-effort was all important because there were few tools and methods. Today the tools and the methods are far more important than man-effort. And the future holds the possibility of a factory where there will be little man-effort, where machinery will do the work, and where men will be paid high wages to sit and push buttons and watch machines.

And in the more complex world to come, far more burdens will fall upon top management than upon the workers. The responsibility for those added burdens should be rewarded, and that is where the incentive effort should be most effective.

Stockholders will pay well for large earnings, whether plowed back into the business for growth or paid out in dividends.

How to work an incentive plan is a matter of opinion. In my view, a modern incentive system should do two things: it should promote teamwork among the management group; and it should reward individual effort, taking into account the desired objectives.

Here is one that I think works pretty well. It is based upon return on investment. We create a pot from earnings. Part of it, say 40 per cent, we pay in proper proportion to each manager for the over-all effort of management. This promotes teamwork; it keeps the different division managers helping one another. The other part of the pot, 60 per cent, is then paid to the managers in amounts based upon their individual performance within their respective divisions.

In measuring this performance, goals are set for each division. The goals are weighted to take into account return on investment, percentage of profit on sales, size of earnings in dollars. That takes account of the larger as compared with the smaller divisions. Weight is also given to improvement in performance, product, and, finally, marketing.

This program gives great flexibility. To promote growth in a new division you can weight the goal for research and product development. In an old division you weight for performance or for profit and efficiency.

In my business there is a new division that one year had a goal of *minus* 10 per cent "profit." The goal was set low so that much could be spent on research and development. An older division was assigned a profit goal of *plus* 20. When above its goal, a division is in black ink; when below, it is in red. Thus, if the new division with a goal of *minus* 10 per cent produced *minus* 9, it was in black ink; whereas, if the division with the goal of *plus* 20 turned in only 19 per cent, it went into red ink.

One other form of incentive that has been effective recently is the granting of stock ownership. Today there is little ownership management. Helping the younger men in the business acquire stock ownership, if feasible, provides a wholesome stimulus. Since we have done this, I have been interested to see how every decision reached by these young men has been determined on the basis of what is best for the company as a whole. They are thinking, you see, of that capital gain they hope to realize someday.

These are just a few of the simple things that some companies have found effective in creating climate. I hope that someday "climate" can be reduced to an exact science! But in the meantime I do know this: that time is short; that the great increase in productivity lies just ahead of us; and that America must have business statesmanship to use it well.

Today expanding industry needs better management, and America needs leadership that can explain and interpret industry. It is the lack of adequate management that is Europe's trouble today — not any lack of resources. On the business leadership of America will fall a great responsibility in the next few years.

EXECUTIVE FREEDOM

Robert W. Johnson

If executive effectiveness were merely a question of charts, instruction, regulation, and definition of authority, the task would be relatively simple. Layouts of administrative structure, analytical reports, and economic data are inert until made alive through men. Executive spirit, therefore, deserves first priority.

At Johnson & Johnson we think more in terms of the intangibles than in terms of the tangibles of executive procedure. To frame the proposition in the opposite sense, little is accomplished through the most perfect concept of organization if its result is the loss of freedom and inspirational expression on the part of the individual executive.

We believe in giving high priority to the establishment and maintenance of individual dignity and prestige, both within the organization and outside it.

By contrast, we have a deathly fear of formality, bureaucracy, red tape, protocol, and any devices leading toward frustration. We are continuously endeavoring through a series of training programs to educate ourselves away from the bureaucratic management concept.

In these days of large and medium-size business, it is easy to have too many problems under one administrative tent, and too many products manufactured under one industrial roof. Therefore, in an attempt to avoid unmanageable and complex integration, and

NOTE: General Johnson is Chairman of the Board, Johnson & Johnson. Because of illness he was unable to present the talk on which this chapter is based. He was represented by Mr. Richard B. Sellars, President, Ethicon Suture Laboratories, a Johnson & Johnson associate company; and some of Mr. Sellars' observations have been included in General Johnson's text.

as a means of increasing executive self-reliance, our company has long pursued a policy of decentralization.

Through decentralization we have developed simplification and provided an opportunity for delegation of executive authority away from central headquarters to the management groups heading the autonomous corporate units that go to make up our family of companies.

The extent to which we are decentralized, so that you may better appreciate the degree of delegation of authority within Johnson & Johnson, is best illustrated by a brief account of our company.

In our 65-year history, we have developed from a centralized administrative and manufacturing unit to both an operating company and a group ownership company. The decentralization plan began back in 1934, when the first affiliate was formed by breaking away certain products from the general line. Throughout the years we have pursued this policy to the point where we now have the operating company which manufactures, sells, and distributes the familiar Johnson & Johnson surgical products, and which is also the owning company of 20 affiliates operating autonomously in the domestic and foreign markets.

Our total employment is only 13,000 — small compared with some of the companies represented in this book — but our operations are spread among 35 plants. So we really do follow the principle of small manageable units. And this, we feel, gives us the best climate for developing practical executives.

The common denominator in increasing executive effectiveness, we believe, is executive freedom on the part of the management people who operate these plants and businesses. Each one of the key executives in the Johnson & Johnson family of companies has had the opportunity early in his experience to learn his job in what we consider the best way — by doing it.

Lest I give the wrong impression, this executive freedom is not provided by putting a man into a job to succeed or fail. It certainly is not like the device a father might use to teach his son to swim — throwing him into the middle of the lake and hoping he would make the shore.

By contrast, we attempt to select our management material carefully, train these men with all the modern devices available to us, and then give them the greatest opportunity to grow in the job, through experience, with plenty of help and guidance, but not with restricting and frustrating controls.

There would be limited value to this philosophy if, as an example, Mr. Sellars, who is president of our Ethicon Suture Laboratories, received the benefit of this executive freedom from the parent company but did not provide the same freedom of operation to the executives within Ethicon. Further, as Mr. Sellars has told me, his own effectiveness would be reduced if he did not draw upon the strength and the creative abilities of his associates.

Thus, within the format of the decentralized organization which of itself has contributed to simplification of procedure, there is further opportunity for executive freedom and the delegation of authority. Each decentralized organization must delegate and adequately deputize within itself. At the same time our executives, although each man has his own clearly understood function, work together in task forces, special committees, and auxiliary boards. These groups operate freely along multiple management lines. They discover, define, and investigate problems. They recommend solutions to top management, and frequently carry them out. These groups go far toward maintaining executive spirit, a company-wide viewpoint, and a willingness among executives to collaborate freely in problem solution, always preserving the individual dignity and freedom of those who serve in coöperative groups.

For 25 years we have operated with product directors, men who are both specialists and generalists. As specialists they know and are responsible for one or a few products. As generalists they carry this responsibility through our purchasing, manufacturing, accounting, research and development, and promotional departments. The product director is a coördinator of the services of these various departments which work in the interests of his product. He carries over-all responsibility for the product. The same over-all responsibility exists for regional sales directors and district sales managers.

We realize, of course, that this administrative structure is not new until we add the ingredient of executive freedom. It is difficult, if not impossible, to define this ingredient on paper, for here we are dealing with an attitude — a state of mind starting at the top, and penetrating throughout the organization.

I think we have learned certain rules of the game that help us to promote this philosophy among our executives. We know that executive freedom cannot be created by edict and that men do not learn by merely being told. It requires years of explanation and example to demonstrate that executive freedom can and will contribute to executive competence.

Perhaps we can define it best by calling it a habit of executive practice, a "state of mind." This cannot take place without a conscious determination to develop such a state of mind. It certainly will not occur automatically.

The policy of executive freedom is not without problems. The most frustrating experience is to stand aside and observe a mistake and to make no move to correct it. But we frequently find that the man making an error discovers it himself, before the mistake comes to full fruition. If he does make this discovery, he has certainly learned a lesson for life. If he is stopped by even the most persuasive executive, he will believe that he was right and, had he been privileged to carry his program to conclusion, all would have been well. At times men do carry mistakes to ultimate failure, but usually these failures are not catastrophic to either the organization or to the men.

What I am describing — what I believe we are practicing to some degree in our companies — is really nothing more than providing opportunities for new experiences through learning by doing, with limited guidance, but freedom of operation to the individual executive.

In addition to the freedom on the job, we provide substantial opportunity for broadening the executive's knowledge of our operations through such devices as special group assignments, job rotation, task forces, and a more formalized program as a means of increasing executive effectiveness.

A device which I am certain is very frequently used, and one that we find valuable, is the formation of a Supervisors' Club. For example, all our people in the New Brunswick area attend a monthly meeting in the evening. An informal talk on some current factor of our operations usually opens the meeting. There follows a break for half an hour of cocktails, and then we sit down together for dinner.

Another customary device is to take various departments within our business and have annual conferences. Thus in Chicago, at the Edgewater Beach Hotel, we plan to hold the Fourth Annual Manufacturing Conference for our Ethicon Suture organization. At that time we will have together the entire supervisory personnel of both the New Brunswick and Chicago plants; there will not be one single supervisory person left in either plant for Thursday, Friday, and Saturday; *but* those plants will continue to operate without any difficulty, judging by the experience of prior years. I think that is a good testimonial to the type of executive freedom that we have in our organization.

Of course, there are many influences working in opposition to our theories of executive freedom. We live in a time of formalized procedure. Some of this grows out of the legislative era, where corrections are attempted through the rigid laws of legislation. Another influence toward highly formalized, defined procedures is the union contract, where in most instances the paragraphs and clauses attempt to cover any and all situations. Another facet of the same design is the pension plan, the insurance plan, the sickness benefit plan, the SEC, the various and sundry bureau requirements such as those of the tax department and other government authority, and so on.

All of this has tended to develop influences in opposition to executive freedom and expression. We are determined that our central administration shall not become an "industrial Pentagon."

Given good administrative housekeeping, adequate financial return, and orderly thinking, we see the stimulant of free expression as one of the great attributes of modern management. We would rather have this spirit of freedom, with its price of occasional error, than the depressing and limiting influence of centralized administration and control.

In a way, we are close to that force that created and developed the United States. As one studies the continuing thread of American history, one senses that it was this desire for free expression and untrammeled opportunity which created our nation in the first instance, and carried it forward thereafter. In giving our modern executive his freedom within the pattern of enlightened coöperation, we are giving him his national inheritance on the modern executive level. Such a gift is beyond price. It is the truest stimulant to self-development. In fact, it *is* development.

EFFICIENT ORGANIZATIONAL STRUCTURE

Ralph J. Cordiner

How can executive effectiveness be increased by efficient organizational structure?

Let me introduce this subject by making some observations about management stewardship, management responsibilities. In General Electric we think of management as being a profession, like engineering or marketing or manufacturing. As such, it has to develop a code of ethics and a background against which it can be measured and judged. It is not just a matter of making money, although I assure you that our directors place that objective high on the list, as also do our shareowners. As I see it, professional managers must consider five different areas that they serve:

1. *The customers* — I completely agree with my coauthors that the customer in the market place where a company offers its product or service is indeed king; and that all the efforts of professional management and all its functional responsibility are obviously directed toward that customer.

2. *The shareowners* — These are the people who have entrusted management with their savings and have made it possible to operate the company.

3. *The employees* — I am thinking of employees at all levels, and of the fact that particular attention should be paid to their dignity as well as to their compensation.

4. *The suppliers* — This area too is important, for the economy is made up of large, medium-size, and small companies, all interdependent.

5. *The public* — I mean the public in its broader sense, including the other four areas that I have listed, but going beyond that; I mean specifically the public toward which the company has a corporate responsibility as a citizen — a responsibility high on the list of the successful professional manager.

NOTE: Mr. Cordiner is President of the General Electric Company.

Now, how can the organizational structure of the company aid the professional manager in discharging these responsibilities? I hasten to point out that my observations from here on may be somewhat provocative. But that may be useful rather than otherwise. Thinking is always stimulated by a reasonable amount of disagreement.

Foremost I feel it is necessary to have written company policies in order to measure an individual manager as to performance. And certainly the man involved has a right to know the company policies which he is supposed to adhere to and on which he is to be measured.

I have in mind no elaborate array of policies, but a small number expressed in concise terms. Possibly the very first policy is the fundamental approach or objective of the company itself. For example, is it the plan of the company to grow through research and advance development within the company, or is it the plan to grow through acquisition of outside companies? The answer to that question must be known to management at all levels.

Another example of fundamental policy concerns decentralized operations. Is it the plan of the company to pay community wage rates or national rates? This is a question that comes up often, and it obviously must be defined in terms of over-all policy.

Or, still another area is that of community contributions and local taxes. What type of corporate citizen should the company try to be? Or take a current matter of discussion and controversy in the American scene—labor legislation. Is it the company policy to remain silent on politically controversial subjects hoping to win by default, or is the company going to take a stand? That, again, has to be an over-all company policy.

Even with complete decentralization, which I shall discuss in a moment, there are certain areas subject to over-all policy. Having consistent rules as to retirement for all employees on the pension plan is one such example. Anything like this, which represents "withheld authority" so far as the decentralized operations are concerned, should be defined; and all members of management, as well as all employees who are interested, should know the company policy about it.

But now let me turn specifically to the major policy of decentralization as we practice it at General Electric. And, since decentralization must start at the top, perhaps it will be clearest if I describe in personal terms what happened when I became president of the company — in December 1950 when my predecessor, Mr. Charles Wilson, was asked to go to Washington as the first Defense Mobilizer.

This all happened in a very short space of time — actually about 48 hours. And at the time of the December board of directors meeting, when the directors were faced with the necessity of electing a successor to Mr. Wilson, I asked if I could say a few words, because I wished to put them on notice that I thought they had enjoyed a disproportionately "good buy" in Charlie Wilson, and that in Cordiner they were not getting the same type of personality. Specifically, Mr. Wilson was a man with tremendous mental and physical stamina, ability to work long hours within the company and long hours outside the company on public service. But I wished the directors to know that I would not try to be Charlie Wilson, for all my great admiration and affection for him; and that my first objective, which I would lay before them in 30 days at the January meeting, would be to decentralize the company, and to start specifically with the president's office.

So in January 1951, one month later — and again I want to emphasize the point that decentralization must start with the chief executive officer — the president's office was detailed into six areas involving the chairman of the board, four group executives (the top executive vice presidents), and the president, each with specified assignments, delegated authority, deputized responsibility.

Then, very promptly, we went further, and delegated at operating levels from 8 former divisions to 24 present divisions, and from 23 former operating departments to 101 operating departments within the divisions.

Now, when I say "delegated," I mean (except for matters of over-all company policy such as I mentioned earlier) complete delegation of authority and responsibility, and also the accountability that must go along with that.

Of course, in a far-flung operation, which is thus delegated into operating areas, there must be some type of mortar to hold the company together. (We think of our operating units as building blocks.) Otherwise these 24 operating divisions and 101 operating departments would be split off in as many different directions. For that reason we have created what we call "services divisions"—for example, the Marketing Services Division and the Manufacturing Services Division, with which are associated Mr. Cutright and Mr. Lewis who are responsible for chapter sections later in this book.

I will not go into all the long and tedious discussions involved in making this transition from our former staff type of organization. It is the results that are important.

Prior to January 1951, the top staff of the company had policy authority for manufacturing, engineering, marketing, and so on. We used to tell the operating people in conferences that they were decentralized and had responsibility for their own operations. But superimposed were the vice presidents of manufacturing, marketing, finance, employee relations, engineering, and so forth, who in fact were prone to exercise line authority in those theoretically decentralized operations.

We eliminated that entirely in 1951 when we created the services divisions. And of course the heads of these services divisions—the senior officers of the company who with the chairman of the board, the president, and the group executives comprise what we call our "Executive Office"—have the responsibility of keeping the company ahead through teaching, acting as catalysts, bringing in outside information, or transplanting information from within the company in their respective functional areas. But they do *not* have any authority to issue orders to the operating people. The operating people accept or reject the services of these senior officers, depending on how well the latter have done their job of organizing and offering their services—of teaching the operating people, really—which is a more difficult job than just ordering something to be done.

Now, let me mention six general principles which we consider fundamental to a decentralized organization — again at the risk of some difference of opinion.

(1) We start first with the firm conviction that there is no "indispensable man" at any level in the company, and that this is particularly true of the chief executive officer. The chief executive officer, if he is discharging his responsibility to the board of directors representing the shareholders, should, within a period of not longer than three years after he has accepted his assignment, have at least three officers equal to or better than himself in performance who could succeed to his position. And within a period of normal tenure of office, say fifteen years, a chief executive officer should be able to submit to the board of directors for their consideration a minimum of six officers, any one of whom could become president or chief executive officer of the company.

We practice that theory. We believe in it. We think it is particularly important that the board should not be trapped into considering only one individual as the next president. We likewise think it is very important — since we do not want to train the five other men of the six who do not become president for our competitors or for other areas of the industry — that there be a number of positions at top level that are virtually as important, are compensated almost on the same level, and carry the same dignity as the position of chief executive officer. Thus, we have created a number of executive vice presidents who act as group executives. The idea is that these men, along with the president and the chairman of the board, should be a team, with each having his own specific responsibilities, yet able to carry the ball or run interference for the other fellow as occasion requires.

(2) Next, we have tried to eliminate all assistants. I know this may be very controversial. I have talked to many men in other companies who look upon the assignment as an assistant as a great opportunity for training. Maybe the practice works differently elsewhere, but for us it has definite weaknesses.

We found that we had too many layers in the company. We think that a great deal of the trouble with direct labor — at the level of the shop — arises because there are too many layers between the people in the shop and the chief executive officer or the senior officers. We have been striving — still without complete success — for only six layers of management if possible, seven as a maximum, between the man in the shop and the chief executive officer. That is not so easy as it sounds; there are a surprising number of layers of management in most companies.

But that was only one reason for trying to dispense with assistants. We also observed that oftentimes when men became assistants (executive assistants or administrative assistants) to some other man, they served there for a number of years and then were passed by at the time of promotion. If you truly are going to have an assistant foreman or assistant superintendent or assistant manager — or assistant to the president — then you should funnel everything through that person; and of course that does not happen. What usually happens is that the assistant becomes almost an errand boy, particularly if he is working for a strong executive, and he has relatively little opportunity to grow.

I know there is room for dispute on this question, but I also know that this is the lesson from our experience. So we are in the midst of giving job descriptions and job assignments to these important people who formerly served as assistants, trying to get them into the stream of the company organization.

(3) We are trying to avoid committees — committees that have an operating function to perform or decisions to make. Committees of this type have several disadvantages. Usually the committee operates at the speed of its least informed member. Or a timid administrator can use the committee as a means of ducking authority or responsibility. Also, committee work can be very time-consuming. At one time each of the senior officers of our company was a member or chairman of as many as seven or eight committees. We now have one committee, and it is advisory in name and fact; we feel that if we are really going to have decentralized authority, we must rely on individuals, not on committee decisions.

(4) Then there is the necessity of having a clear definition of company policy, which I discussed earlier.

(5) Another basic principle, essential to decentralization, is that

executives at all levels must have confidence in people. It is significant that during the war, when we had no other choice, we elected to have confidence in untried people, and then, to our great satisfaction, we found that they discharged their obligations admirably.

When we were asked to take on the assignment of jet engines for the Air Force, we deliberately staffed that operation with young people. The vice president and general manager of that operation is still in his forties — and he is an old gray-haired man in comparison with the rest of them. The average age of the engineering organization for that intricate product is less than 35 years.

(6) Finally, the organization structure is never complete. It is a vast mistake to think that all that has to be done is to issue some papers and some charts, and that then you can lay the job aside. Changing social or economic conditions, changing trends of the business, the necessity of implementing or emphasizing a new and growing area, all necessitate the recognition that the organization structure is always flexible. And to that end we have created internally what we call "management consultation services," to be certain that we do not lose sight of the necessity of staying flexible.

I realize that these observations may be suspect without any figures to back them up. The natural reaction may be: "Well, that is all very interesting. Cordiner has some personal theories. Perhaps he has been able to force them on the General Electric Company. Possibly he has been successful in having a board of directors support them in the first instance."

So let me qualify myself as a witness and describe the factual results. What has been accomplished in these last three years is the real payoff.

I shall have to put this in terms of billions, but please do not think of it that way. Think of it in terms of these 101 operating departments of ours where the authority resides — or of the 150 or whatever it may be that we shall have as we grow. For we must get our operations down into smaller and smaller components — to a size where a manager can get his arms around it; it is just as simple as that. This business of billions is all relative, anyway; a business measured in the thousands has most of the same problems.

With that much for a premise, let me point out that in 1950 our sales were just short of $2,000,000,000, and that without entering into any new business or without acquiring any companies in the last three years — because one of our policies is to grow from within the company, through research and advance development — the first four months of 1953 were 76 per cent ahead of the first four months of 1950. In terms of tonnage, where there is no inflation, the increase is slightly more than 60 per cent in the three years.

Then, of course, the thing that seems to interest all professional management — and is part of the fun of the game — is that figure in the southeast corner of the operating statement: the net profit. Using pretax figures, because taxes were different in 1950 from what they are today, our average annual earnings for the three-year period since 1950 are 97 per cent ahead of 1950.

Moreover, our percentage of the available business has never been so high in the 30 years that we have kept a record. And it is also significant — taking market price as value — that our stock has gone from 47⅛ to a recent price of 75 on the New York Stock Exchange. (And I am not trying to sell any stock, let the Securities and Exchange Commission take note!)

Finally, during this period, through this decentralized organization, we have been able to carry on physical expansion at a rate of $150 million a year of company expenditures, without any borrowing or new equity financing, and we have three more years of that program still ahead of us.

But most important is the fact that decentralization — breaking the job down into these divisions and departments and sections, and delegating the assignments — brought opportunity to hundreds, yes thousands, of General Electric men. There is nothing that gives as much of a thrill or satisfaction to any of us in professional management as to accord to our associates the opportunity of growth, the dignity of the position, and the satisfaction of accomplishment.

That part of it has meant more to us in the Executive Office than any of these figures I have just cited.

PART II

HOW TO DEVELOP GENERAL MANAGERS

Lyndall F. Urwick, Clarence B. Caldwell, and Mark W. Cresap, Jr.

In the brief space allotted I propose to limit myself to certain somewhat dogmatic statements. However, the dogmatism is a mechanical convenience — since qualifications are so cumbersome — and does not represent the spirit in which I submit my ideas.

For over a year I have been engaged in an inquiry on behalf of the American Management Association into executive development, a research project entitled, "A Study of Management Education for Itself and Its Employees."

Almost every leading executive to whom I have talked, particularly in the larger corporations, has emphasized the difficulty of developing general managers. By this they have usually meant asking a man in the middle forties, who has spent the previous 20 years climbing the ladder in some one of the specialized functions characteristic of current business organization, to assume over-all responsibility as executive vice president or as president. And I get the impression that the presidential ranks are full of ex-vice presidents of manufacturing who cannot sell what they can make or of ex-vice presidents of marketing who cannot make what they can sell, or of ex-general counsel who only feel thoroughly at home when the corporation is involved in or avoiding litigation. Less facetiously, there is no doubt about the need for broad-gauged men.

The well-deserved popularity of the Advanced Management Pro-

NOTE: Lt. Col. Urwick is Chairman, Urwick, Orr & Partners, Ltd., London, England; Mr. Caldwell is Vice President and Director of Personnel, Sears, Roebuck and Company; and Mr. Cresap is Vice President — Assistant to the President, Westinghouse Electric Corporation.

The introduction and conclusion are based on Lt. Col. Urwick's observations, and the two accounts of company practice represent the experiences of Mr. Caldwell and Mr. Cresap.

gram at the Harvard Business School (and now in more and more other universities) is one symptom of the need that is felt for some broadening process. But that very popularity may combine with the urgency of current requirements to distract attention from a more farsighted attack on the problem. "Operation Stopgap" may create obstacles to a proper consideration of "Operation Future." Prestige has its pitfalls. The *average* age of the men in the 1952 AMP course at Harvard, for example, was 48. And I can see the day when it may be impossible to secure admission to the course unless the candidate is *already* a president or president-designate in need of an intellectual aperient to clear the mental constipation produced by too much specialization.

Here are two little bits of evidence that current requirements are urgent:

(1) While there are few satisfactory figures, it is manifest to ordinary observation that the health of high business executives in this country needs looking at. Premature casualties from ulcers, hearts, nervous exhaustion, and similar occupational diseases are well above the national average. The "rat-race" is killing a lot of irreplaceable rats — which is exactly what one would expect if rats are encouraged to indulge in long-distance racing without adequate examination before they start or any satisfactory scheme of training.

(2) I know of management consultants — colleagues of mine in this country — who are specializing in advising presidents on their *personal* problems. And they have a large staff.

It is not only difficult but impossible, except in rare instances, to turn a specialist into a generalist unless the process is *started* far earlier in life than business in this country has hitherto contemplated. Hollywood realized this a long time ago. They have a saying, "You cannot groom elderly spinsters for stardom." There are the rare cases which nothing will stop. But my concern is not with the exceptions; rather it is focused on:

a. Raising the national average of general management performance.

b. Saving some substantial percentage of the irreplaceable experience which is at present being quite unnecessarily wasted through overstrain.

Fortunately, the same device, if it is understood and applied, can be used to deal with both desiderata. In relieving high executives of much of the routine which keeps them incurably desk-bound we can create positions which will provide the necessary training ground for coming generations of general managers.

Perhaps it can be agreed that there are two major elements in the development of any general manager. He must:

a. Keep his mental processes alive and expanding. This will give him intellectual and, in part, social breadth.

b. Have appropriate "on the job" experience supported by the best possible coaching. This will deepen character and develop wisdom — and this is by far the more important of the two elements.

The first half of the problem presents few difficulties. Business must only abandon its traditional "Humpty Dumpty" attitude toward the educational process. Too many boys go to college and obtain a qualification (whatever that means) and then fall off the academic wall into practical life, where "all the Queen's horses and all the Queen's men" will never persuade them to open a book again. All they can hope to gain from a few short years at a university is to "learn how to learn." The vital point about the educational process is that it should be continuous to the grave. If the preparation given to the young men of the United States in its passionately endowed educational institutions does not achieve this elementary requirement, it is up to business, which, after all, has every kind of opportunity to influence the national pattern of education, to see that that preparation is changed.

On its own side of this half of the problem, the main responsibility of business is to ensure that the educational process, once started, is not checked by too much "rat-racing." There are at least two climacterics in the intellectual evolution of every young man worth worrying about in this context. The first usually occurs somewhere between 27 and 35 years of age. At this point a man suitable to go to the top should be forced to pause for a substantial period; I think a year is not too long. He should be sent back to the books and the theory, be relieved of the routine, and, above all, be given *time* for thought and reflection. He should be made to realize that sometime in the not very distant future he will be required to cross a mental crevasse — the immense difference in method between managing people and things that he can meet face-to-face, that he can touch and see, and administering groups of human beings from a distance, through other people.

The second climacteric occurs later, usually sometime between 38 and 45 years of age. Again the individual has to cross a mental crevasse. He is coming to the point when he will be required to exercise top leadership in some business institution. Quite suddenly he will have to change his whole outlook. It will no longer be sufficient for him to be a competent professional concerned with the internal administrative problems of his institution, skilled in dealing with the social group to which he is accustomed. His main preoccupation will be to relate that institution to the environment in which it is set. And that, in this country today, means not only to the continental United States and to Washington; it also means to the far corners of the seven seas and to "men of every clime and color." Again he needs a pause for thought and reflection. Though, at this stage, I imagine that six months is a sufficient investment in a necessarily limited individual future.

Provided business will realize and face up to the need for these pauses if intellectual development is to be continuous, I have little doubt that appropriate instructional machinery can be worked out by business and our wealth of educational institutions acting in collaboration.

The second half of the problem — providing suitable "on the job" experience and high-level coaching in leadership is both more important and more recalcitrant. The first thing every bright young man is told on joining a business corporation is that he lacks "practical experience." Business is young in the art of executive development; it has less than half a century of practical experience in handling really large numbers in its institutions. The armies of the world have had practical experience with this problem for close on to one hundred times that period. And in all advanced communities they have arrived at the same solution. They train future generals — the same word as general managers — by employing specially selected and trained individuals as "*general* staff officers," that is as "assistants to" a high executive in carrying out his functions of direction and leadership.

While there are differences which must be taken into account between the purposes and conditions of military as opposed to business organizations, I have no doubt as to the basic principle involved. This military plan has two immense advantages:

(1) Picked younger men are given an opportunity, while their minds are still comparatively flexible, of thinking about and dealing with problems of general management. By definition they are not yet ready to carry its moral responsibilities; they are not required to do so.

(2) They are given direct coaching by the men who are the leaders of the profession, not by some subordinate who is working out his time. Leadership is example, and men can only learn to lead through direct contact with the best examples. A Pershing makes a Marshall, and a Marshall makes an Eisenhower.

The problem of providing such "on the job" experience in business is a difficult one because it involves something of a revolution in business thought about organization. Business has become overspecialized and has consequently given too much status to its top specialists. Business is "lousy" with vice presidents in special staff functions. It has, in consequence, depreciated both the status and the authority of the *line* positions, the positions which contribute daily and directly to profit, as opposed to the positions which are merely ancillary to the central purpose of the undertaking. In many corporations the "chain of command" is totally obscured by a tangle of service activities.

Each of the incumbents of these special staff positions is a "natural" obstacle to the creation of correct "general staff" posts. They are not to be blamed for being human. They claim competence and authority for *their* particular function as all human beings are prone to do. But they are overwhelming general management. Presidents and executive vice presidents are being worked into early graves by problems of coördination. And when they seek relief by appointing "assistants to" themselves, too often a Camorra of vice presidents plots an immediate assassination. The post of "assistant to" the president is a hissing and a reproach in scores and hundreds of corporations in the United States today.

Yet, until such posts are properly established, the problem of developing general managers will not be solved. For American business will lack the positions in which potential leaders can gain *practical* experience in the problems of general management and learn leadership from the best examples *while they are still young enough* to benefit from such opportunities. And, until such opportunities are created inside business, nothing that can be done by way of courses of instruction at universities, junior boards, job rotation, and so on will prove wholly effective. These devices for developing people intellectually are valuable. But they only deal with half, and that the least important half, of the problem.

Now let us look at what two great American companies are doing to develop general managers.

Sears, Roebuck and Co.

Any discussion of executive development at Sears should begin with a brief background of our executives themselves.

To begin with, the typical Sears executive is a young man—younger than most who carry comparable responsibility in the competitive world of business. Our early retirement age—63 years—is one of the reasons we can bring young men up in our organization. When a key executive retires, a large number of promotions result all along the line, and many younger men have an opportunity to accept greater responsibility.

In spite of their relative youth, however, most Sears executives are veterans of many years of Sears training. This is primarily true because of our policy of promotion from within. Over the years, we have found that, by looking to our own ranks first for promotable talent, we can accomplish two important objectives: we can provide incentive for those who wish to rise, and we can do a better job of selection among men whose backgrounds have become well known to us during their initial years of service.

Because they have had sufficient opportunity to prove their worth, and for other important reasons that we will cover later, the typical Sears executives are loyal. For example, at the conclusion of the war in 1945, we had over 17,000 people in military service, on leave from our company. Of these, 13 per cent were commissioned officers. At the conclusion of their military service, *96 per cent of these men returned to Sears,* allowing us to take men back into our organization who had been away for four, five, or six years; men who had, during that time, assumed greater responsibilities than they might have assumed during their entire lives in a business organization.

It was on this group of young veterans that we depended most importantly for our explosive expansion program — a program which involved the expenditure of $450 million in the establishment of new stores, enlargement of old stores, the building of a mail order plant and certain factory installations, our South American expansion program, and, more recently, our expansion into the Dominion of Canada.

With this background in mind, let me go on to discuss, not the mechanics of our program at Sears, but the over-all personnel philosophy which serves as the essential framework for our executive development program.

Executive effectiveness is a product of an adequate, well-rounded and thoroughly consistent personnel program. Here, as we see it, are some of the characteristics which this kind of a personnel program must have:

(1) Most important, the personnel program should have the *full and enthusiastic support of the company's top management.* By this I mean far more than mere lip service. I mean that the officers of the corporation should be prepared to make the kinds of decisions and to take the kind of action that a comprehensive personnel program calls for. In a large company, these decisions and these actions involve the expenditure of many millions of dollars. They involve difficult choices between the hard realities of conducting a competitive business and the equally urgent responsibilities for treating its men and women like 1953-style American citizens.

(2) This brings me to another essential characteristic of a sound personnel program — *the way a company treats its people.* I am thinking here of both human and economic values.

In *human values* I include the dignity of the individual. This means that we must make men and women feel that they belong, that they are a very real and important part of the group. This also means that we must take people into our confidence, share our problems with them, encourage them to speak out and to help in the making of decisions.

The *economic values* encompass a variety of things. One of the most important of these, of course, is wages. A corporation such as Sears meets its wage obligations by paying a 20 per cent higher average wage than the nationwide average for retailing as a whole. But this is only one facet of economic security. In addition to "buying an employee's time," a sound personnel policy must provide an adequate program of *incentive benefits*.

At Sears, for example, in 1952 our benefit program cost $900 per employee — or 42 cents per hour, over and above wages, throughout the year. These benefits not only include hospitalization insurance, vacations with pay, a paid sickness allowance of ten weeks per year, and other standard benefits; they also include unusual benefits such as our medical catastrophe insurance plan whereby an employee who suffers a prolonged illness, or who has a serious accident, can receive as much as $5,000 to defray his expenses. And these benefits include, in the case of Sears, a profit-sharing plan which has enabled 118,000 employees to become the owners of 26 per cent of the company's stock — stock which each employee continues to own when he retires or leaves the company. Some retirees are collecting a greater annual sum in profit-sharing stock dividends alone than their annual salaries amounted to while they were working.

Providing the employee with a feeling of security in both the human and the economic areas is certainly an indispensable characteristic of a sound and forward-looking personnel program. But, there are still other important characteristics of such a personnel program.

(3) High on the list I would place the kind of *climate* or *atmosphere* which puts a premium upon the man who is courageous but, at the same time, is able to discipline himself for teamwork; and upon the man of ability who is, at the same time, not unwilling to learn. This kind of climate refuses to reward political maneuvering. It seeks out, and, if necessary, liquidates the man who tries to make his own way at the expense of others and at the expense of the company. It has no room for the man who thinks that the way to get ahead is to "play it smart," to "know the angles," and to manipulate his fellows.

(4) There is one final characteristic of a good personnel program which I should like to mention. It is simply this — that a company and its policies never stand still. In our fast-moving, dynamic American society, companies are constantly changing, developing, and improving.

Just as they improve their products and their service to customers, they must constantly improve their personnel program. Show me a company which is perfectly satisfied with its personnel program and I will be concerned for that company's future.

A corporation's most precious asset is the morale of its people. A sound personnel program harbors this asset, guards it jealously, and constantly seeks better ways of discharging its responsibility toward this asset. In such a company, I personally would be thoroughly unworried about executive effectiveness.

Executive effectiveness begins with the original *selection* of the young man who is your future executive. Our experience has shown that the judgments one can form of a candidate in a personal interview need to be supplemented by the scientific accuracy of a battery of psychological tests. Such a battery should give you not only a pretty accurate estimate of a man's mental horsepower but also a comprehensive picture of his personality. We have found, too, that it is desirable to retest a man as he moves up in the organization. All of us undergo changes as we have new experiences.

Let me emphasize that we use tests only as an adjunct to our appraisals — but an important adjunct. We do not assign a man to a major job unless he has had the tests. All those who take part in his appraisal — following the regular routine of rating forms — must formalize their personal opinions before the results of the testing are made known. Then the tests are used to impersonalize these personal opinions, if I may put it that way — to affirm or deny the fact that the man in question has the qualifications indicated by the personal opinions.

As a result, we are trying to be more and more objective, rather than letting subjective judgments sway us unduly in our selections of men for advancement. At the same time, we are careful not to go too far — not to allow the tests to be abused as they would be if we used them for firing or demoting, not to have them used as a political football, not to consider them a complete substitute for judgment or a means of outguessing the normal selection process. That would mean the loss of the great potentialities of tests in helping to select just the right individual — and not a stereotype — for advancement to the right position.

The proper *placement* of executives is essential to their effectiveness. An excellent man in the wrong assignment can do grave damage not only to himself but to the company. We have found the judicious use of our psychological testing battery, as described, most important in placing our executives in the most rewarding assignments. One has to know of an individual how well he can work with other people; one has to know whether he is the type of man who can stand up under considerable pressure day after day or whether, instead, he would do his best work in the relatively relaxed atmosphere of a research department. Is he a man who can provide leadership or does he make a better follower? How important is economic gain in his life? How well can he take criticism? How well can he give criticism? A large company such as Sears has a very wide variety of jobs, and it is just elementary that we should use every device we can to make sure that people are in assignments for which they are best fitted and which best fit them.

In addition, we also consider *rotation* of assignments to be essential in increasing executive effectiveness. Serving in a number of capacities as he progresses in the company, an executive not only gains additional job know-how, he also develops what is perhaps the most essential ingredient of executive effectiveness — breadth of perspective. The closer to the top a man moves, the more essential it becomes for him to develop breadth of perspective — to take a less and less provincial view of problems.

In developing a man who gives promise of becoming a general manager, for instance, we would not hesitate to take him from any position to rotate him in the types of jobs necessary for him to gain experience. Generally we would try to get the man into a position where he would not be working in his normal environment. This would enable other people to appraise his qualifications and give him the broadening that would come from his new association, and also would challenge his ingenuity to adjust to new situations.

This development that a man undergoes on the job depends on a number of factors. Very important among these is the *administrative structure* of the organization. The structure reflects the climate of the whole personnel program which I mentioned earlier. If the climate is democratic, if it is one in which individuals are held to be important in and of themselves, the administrative structure will allow jobs to be molded to men. It will allow a man to express in his job the full flavor of his own unique personality.

At Sears, we say that we have a "flat" organization. There are only four levels of supervision between the rank-and-file worker in a store and the president of the company. A short time ago a number of professors of administrative law came to visit us from Turkey. They were considerably surprised at the fact that we quite frequently have as many as 50 or 60, or even 100 men, reporting to a single vice president. They were troubled by the absence of echelons. So we explained to them that the vice president had budgeting figures, market reports, a merchandise development laboratory, a shopping service, and so on, as supplementing aids; that the men reporting to him enjoyed considerable autonomy, made their own decisions, and worked out their own plans; and that as a consequence a conference once in three months concerning the general, fundamental problems involved in his department was enough to provide positive direction. Then these professors realized that what they were looking at was a basic philosophy, a basic climate, in which democracy is at a premium.

Beyond the proper selection, the proper placement, the proper rotation, and the proper freedom of executives, I must mention one further factor that contributes to executive efficiency — and this is *education*. Education is a broad term and covers a very wide variety of activities. It includes the formal education which an executive might receive in the advanced management division of a school, such as Harvard Business School. It includes formal classes, or courses, or institutes, or seminars — call them what you will — which a corporation conducts on its own premises for selected executives. It includes participation in the kind of conferences on which this book is based. It includes service on committees of all kinds. It includes the leadership of discussion groups as well as the training of other men.

In the development of our own executives we have used all of these techniques. Last year we added another — economic education. This is an effort to broaden the basic information and the viewpoint of our executives in matters of general public affairs, with particular reference to the competitive system of business which we have been developing in this country over the years.

The fact that ours is a fast-moving, dynamic society cannot be overemphasized. Business executives will be truly effective only when they have acquired the know-how, the insight, and the skill to exercise competent leadership in our changing times. Business is no longer isolated from society — if, indeed, it ever was. It is part and parcel of society. And the effective executive is a man who is as familiar with the affairs of his world as he is with the affairs of his corporation.

Westinghouse Electric Corporation

The earlier part of this book is devoted to considering the proper climate for the growth of executives, the organizational philosophy and management policies that will encourage the natural development of talent. This part of the book is intended to complement these ideas by extending the discussion to the matter of the techniques of executive development — with special reference, in this chapter, to the development of general managers.

At the outset it is necessary to define the term "general manager" in the sense in which I use it, in order to avoid any subsequent confusion. This definition, of course, will reflect the circumstances existing in the particular organization to which I belong. When speaking of a general manager position, I refer to a position carrying direct responsibility for profit, usually a profit on a product line or group of lines, and normally incorporating the execution of the basic functions of sales, engineering, and manufacturing. Such a position in the Westinghouse Electric Corporation is comparable to the responsibility of a president in firms competing directly and primarily in the same market as the lines for which our respective general managers are responsible. There are approximately fifty of such positions in our company, ranging from the general manager of a small department with an annual volume of about two million dollars to the president, with the responsibility for a volume of about one and one-half billion dollars.

In referring to the "responsibility for profit," I mean the profit produced in relation to the assets, both fixed and current, which are employed in producing that profit. This responsibility is not only for volume and margin but also for asset utilization and turnover. Thus, the key performance of measure applied to our general managers is the rate of return on assets.

What abilities, what understanding, what knowledge must a man possess to discharge these responsibilities successfully?

This question breaks down into two parts: (1) What inherent and personal attributes are required? (2) What types of understanding and knowledge can be acquired in the course of a man's development through experience, education, and training?

In approaching the first question — inherent characteristics — we encounter the fuzziest and most nebulous element of the problem. We at Westinghouse have not solved it to our satisfaction; and, frankly, I know of no organization which has.

The starting point is relatively easy — to set forth the bill of requirements in terms of most of the characteristics a man should possess to be a good general manager. In recently refining our bill of requirements, we borrowed heavily on the accumulated knowledge of the Harvard Business School, and on the experience of some other companies. Let me list the ten resulting characteristics briefly, observing that they typify nothing new or unusual, though they have been subject to a great deal of thought and consideration:

1. Demonstrated ability to produce results.
2. Demonstrated ability to get things done through others, by (a) proper handing of people; (b) effectiveness of expression; (c) personality.
3. Mental alertness and capacity for quick understanding.
4. Resourcefulness and originality.
5. Initiative and energy.
6. Ability to profit from experience — capacity for growth.
7. Motivation — desire to improve and succeed.
8. Emotional stability and adaptability.

9. Character — loyalty, sincerity, ethics, and courage.
10. A good health outlook.

Note that these characteristics are termed "inherent"; that is, for the most part they cannot be acquired. Management development programs often overlook the fact that the principal attributes for success fall in this category. Take the matter of the ability to make decisions, which is dependent on many characteristics but will not be present unless a man possesses courage and initiative; there is very little an organization can do to develop these traits in men unless the basic ingredients are built in.

Now, when we come to the question of the means of judging men as regards these characteristics, the clouds begin to thicken. Our experience has returned us to the conclusion that the best method, though far from perfect, is to rely on pooled judgments of people familiar with the makeup and performance of the men in question. In our company a formal appraisal of a man's potential is made annually by the man's supervisor and two of the supervisor's coördinate associates who work closely with that man; the rating is then reviewed with the supervising rater's superior. Through this arrangement we hope to have minimized bias and snap judgments.

Admittedly, this is a very rough means of evaluation, and one which produces many inconsistencies and inequities. I do believe, however, that it enables us to inventory men with outstanding potential sufficiently well to serve the primary purposes of our Management Development Program. We are examining other means of validating appraisals by this method. We are also experimenting with testing, and are incorporating certain tests which are applicable to certain characteristics, but these of course are employed only as supplements to human judgment.

Now, as to the second question — what understanding and knowledge should a man be exposed to in an effort to develop him toward the position of general manager — it seems to me that there are three such fields of understanding and knowledge:

1. Understanding and knowledge of all basic functions embraced by the general managership toward which a man is aimed — to minimize the problem of the unrounded specialist in a generalist position.

2. Understanding and knowledge of management practices—distinguishing the functions of management (dealing with people, organizing, planning, controlling, analytical thinking) from the operating classifications of functions (sales, manufacturing, engineering, etc.).

3. Understanding and knowledge of entrepreneurial strategy and tactics—how to make the greatest profits on the least investments—and I mean sound, growing profits and not those induced by shortsighted milking. I refer to an understanding and knowledge that measures growth not in terms of output or square footage of space but in terms of dividends.

How should a company go about the job of imparting such understanding and of exposing such knowledge to its potential general managers?

We concluded, in our company, that the first thing was to select a relatively small group of high potential people for rather intensive attention. We believe it is important to avoid the dissipation of development efforts through excessive coverage, depriving the entire program of the selective and individual character. Unless the development efforts are focused on a relatively small group, the program becomes entangled with procedure and suffers from the defects of the quantity approach versus the quality approach.

I do not advocate, nor is it the policy of our company, to neglect the application of means of personal development to our employee group as a whole; we have extensive programs available to all. However, we do distinguish between these latter efforts and the more intensive, careful, and individual cultivation of those who appear to possess high potential for top jobs.

Accordingly, we maintain a "management reserve" inventory of such men in a sufficient number to represent about twice the requirements for management positions (including all "general management" positions) to be filled in the next five years. This "management reserve" numbers about 850 people. To this group we apply certain programs:

1. *Planned rotation of these men to broaden their experience*—We make temporary assignments, of six months to two years, to other functions or to different types of responsibility within the same function.

The procedure of rotating across functional lines is generally practical only with respect to nonsupervisory personnel, or the lower levels of supervision. Higher supervisory personnel can be rotated within their respective functions relatively easily, but it is not usually feasible to give them temporary duty in a position of comparable importance in another function, because of the difficulty of discharging the responsibilities of such a position without prior exposure to that function.

2. *Formal courses in company management policies and practices* — One such course is conducted each year for about 50 men in a two-week session, held at a central location.

3. *Educational courses in the principles of business policy and general management* — Two such courses are conducted by the company each year in a central location, with the enrollment in each course at about 25. These courses are conducted by experienced teachers from graduate business school faculties during the summer recess.

4. *Advanced management program courses at Harvard, University of Pittsburgh, Columbia, and elsewhere* — We participate in these to the extent of about 20 men each year.

5. *A new program which has been evolved in consultation with the Harvard Business School* — I refer to a new course to be conducted during a sixteen-month uninterrupted period but consisting of the regular two-year master in business administration curriculum, in which men with five to seven years' business experience, or its equivalent, will be enrolled. We shall send 15 men to the first session of this course, which commences in February 1954. The men will be very carefully selected on the basis of the ten characteristics which I have already mentioned.

Our purpose in utilizing this course is to expose men with high potential for management to a comprehensive education in the fundamentals of business and general management, at a stage in their company career when they (a) have acquired enough experience and business maturity to enable them to profit considerably more from such training than would be possible immediately following their undergraduate education; and (b) have not become too fixed in outlook and thinking habits to receive full benefit of this type of education.

The preceding five programs are aimed at the three fundamental types of understanding and knowledge, as mentioned earlier, which potential general managers should and can acquire through experience, education, and training as a part of the company's executive development program.

There is one great and dominant challenge to business in its approach to the development of management executives — the revitalization of the entrepreneurial point of view and the culture of its understanding among men of management potential. Trends in business organization and personnel policy of the past two decades have encouraged the adoption of personal career and business philosophies which, if they continue to spread, will take a good deal of the spark out of American industry. I refer to the security-conscious and conformist attitude which guides an increasing number of young men in business today. This is accompanied by greater specialization of education and experience, depriving men, particularly in big companies, of an integrated understanding of the principles of business — of the elements that make up profits.

The entrepreneur is not governed by consideration of security, does not always conform, and knows the key to business profits. Not everyone, of course, can or should aspire to the role of entrepreneur, but more attention should be paid to his point of view in the field of management development if it is to be prevented from becoming obsolete. The maintenance of the private profit system is dependent on what corporate managements do *within* their own organizations, in addition to other factors more fully recognized.

Conclusion

The foregoing discussion raises several questions which require further attention.

As I stated earlier, the great popularity of the advanced management courses organized by some of the universities is a sign that business recognizes the necessity of doing what it can for men approaching the top end of their curve of activity and getting on with it quickly. But this is an emergency operation, put in much too late in the executive's life for the very best results.

Fortunately, we have many executives in business who have a natural genius for the job and who do manage, without any formal plan, to do a great deal of coaching of their successors. But, quite bluntly — and I think we must face this issue — any man over 40 years old who has not had the benefit of deliberate management development from the time he was 22 or 23, is handicapped as compared with a young man of the next generation who will be watched carefully and developed systematically all the way up.

This creates two problems — one for the older man as the younger man begins to press him; and one for the younger man who has been selected as his successor and has been given what is sometimes called "the Crown Prince treatment."

The fact that the older man lacks or has lacked the opportunity in the past which now is provided by the new philosophy, the new vision of business, is of course no reason to discount either his performance or his personality.

I think one of the lessons we have all got to learn from the armed forces is the importance of distinguishing status from function. Function is determined by appointment; rank or status is determined not only by a man's current appointment but also by the whole of his past service. Where a man by virtue of good service in the past has status, younger men must learn that while they may surpass him in function, they can at least pay him the respect which his past deserves.

It is very important, not that the young men should do exactly what the older men will tell them to do, nor that the older men should retain functions which they have outgrown, but that no younger man should be tolerated for five minutes if he cannot recognize that a man with 35 years' good service in a corporation, and responsible executive positions behind him, even though he may perhaps have gone over the top of the curve of his immediate usefulness, is deserving of the respect which is due to his past record.

It is not difficult for younger men to show respect for a record of achievement, and I sometimes deeply regret that we have not yet evolved in business the well-known device of rank which insures that.

I am quite sure that someday business will be forced to do what the fighting services have found necessary in all countries: to distinguish between these two concepts. And any younger man who dares to be impertinent to a man of higher status because he is on his way out will be made to realize very clearly that the day will come when he will be on his way out, too.

Now, what about the effect on the younger men of someone being tapped on the shoulder early for advancement. I have heard the fear expressed that this will limit the initiative and hope of advancement of those not so tapped; and that the younger man who gets this special treatment may have some human relations problems with his fellow workers.

Of course the "Crown Prince" difficulty is aggravated now by the fact that we are at the beginning of this management development upsurge. It is only about five years old so far as any real breadth of interest in this country is concerned. Consequently there are very few men who have so far been given such special opportunity of further training; and when they go back to their corporations, they are "marked men," isolated people.

The fact remains that this is a universal human problem. The men who are picked out from their regiments to go to the Staff College in the British Army, as a result of very severe competitive examinations, have often found their colleagues looking down their noses at them when they got back to their regiments again. Having been rather carefully selected, they usually have had broad enough shoulders to take some of that treatment and to handle it with poise. To learn to do so is part of their training.

So I do not think we can ever get rid of this problem completely; the younger man selected for management development is always going to be considered something of a "Crown Prince." But I do think, as the opportunity for training broadens for the younger men, those who are selected will not feel so different, so much in the minority.

At the same time, there are going to be many younger men who do not succeed in their rise to the top. My own feeling is that to get one future manager at the top, you have to start with three or four at the lower levels of the pyramid; not just one or two, as others seem to think. The casualties on the way up are very much higher than most of us realize, because we all of us forget the misfortunes that happen to our friends and think only in terms of our own expectation of life.

But I still think it is worth while to undertake their development. The whole philosophy behind management development, as has been made clear in the description of the Westinghouse program, rests on a high degree of selection. The implication is that the level approach, the approach of including everybody as a potential candidate for a job, would be a lazy and deadening approach; it would weaken incentive and lead to mediocrity in management.

Now, let us look at this problem of management development more generally. I wish it were possible to provide an accurate picture of this great wave of interest in management development which has swept across United States business in the last four or five years, as I have seen it through my A.M.A. study. Space makes that impossible. However, it may be worth while to highlight several of the more significant findings.

The first has already been stated. We must not be deflected by the urgency of the problem and by the immediate measures we must take to help the men with whom we started too late.

The next point goes even farther. It is not enough to be concerned with the problem from the date at which we recruit new entrants to our great corporations; we must go behind that, to the influence which business must and should bring to bear on our business schools to insure that no man comes out of a business school with a degree who has not had a basic general education. There are some such men escaping into American business at the moment — and that is a situation that cries out for attention.

The business schools have evolved out of commerce by economics; and, owing to the traditional structure of university organizations, business is being studied in almost all universities in at least six to eight different faculties.

If we want to train specialists — engineers, chemists, and so on — of course there must be separate faculties. But what we are concerned with here is the basic training of future businessmen. And I feel very strongly that one of the steps forward that should be taken sometime in the next five or ten years is a real nationwide conference of business people and educators to see if that mixed university pattern of faculties cannot be pulled together into a coherent single faculty bearing on business and preparation for business.

At the same time, I have a certain apprehension that the mechanisms provided by the social sciences will have too much weight put on their shoulders before those shoulders are really broad enough to bear it. It is highly attractive to have an apparently scientific technique for settling some of the real headaches which face executives. But it would be quite fatal if we were to start using some of these techniques before they are ready to give us a true and precise result.

Take the matter of tests. Tests are admittedly useful *as a supplement* to the selection process. But there is always the type of executive who will try to duck his responsibility in choosing men because he knows how wrong we all can go. Dr. Johnson once said, "God Almighty, sir, does not propose to judge man until the end of his days." We can have all the devices of tests, collective opinion analyses, and so on that we can bring to bear on this difficult problem, but we still make the most ghastly mistakes. When we do, it is a great temptation to say "Well, the psychologist said so-and-so,"— to try to evade *our* responsibility as executives by throwing it onto the shoulders of some specialist or some "system."

Perhaps this little story from England will serve to illustrate the role of such techniques as psychological tests:

The traditional old lady came up to an old judge at a dog show, and said, "Mr. Jones, I can't think how you do it. All these little dogs look to me just alike." The old man tilted his cap up and scratched the back of his head, and he said, "Well, you see, lady, it's like this. There may be a score of little dogs in the ring; their owners walk them around and I look at their points. I say to myself, 'This one doesn't carry himself quite as he should — no.' 'Those hindquarters on that one — no.' 'Awful short in the back — no.' But when I have sized up all their points, there may be two, three little dogs that I can't fault. Then I put their heads between my hands and I look them in the eye, and I say to myself, 'George, which of these little dogs would you like to take home?' That's the one that gets the prize, lady."

I do think, whatever we do about developing more scientific techniques, that not in the lifetime of any of those reading this, or of their grandchildren, shall we have techniques in these new sciences which will relieve the executive of the responsibility of putting people's heads between his hands, making up his own mind about them, and standing by the results.

Finally, let me say that of course it would give me infinite delight if the interest in and concern for management in Great Britain was one-tenth as vivid as it is in this great country.

This interest in executive development is not a fad. It is not something which removal of the excess profits tax or even a severe business depression will stop. Retrenchment would only cut off "the lunatic fringe" — the people who are doing it merely because it is fashionable, because everybody else is doing it, and who have not thought out a philosophy for it.

Actually, this upsurge of interest in management development in the serious corporations is the logical conclusion of a realization which has been growing and growing and growing in American business ever since the beginning of this century: the realization that neither equipment nor patents nor markets nor any inanimate thing is worth a damn; that it is not things which make businesses great, but people. Unless we concentrate our first attention on men and women, we have not begun to have a modern philosophy of management.

HOW TO DEVELOP SALES EXECUTIVES

Harry R. Tosdal, A. A. Stambaugh, H. G. Cutright, James C. Olson, and Harry L. Hansen

The problem of developing sales executives has two important aspects. The first and foremost of these concerns the selection of the right men; the second, of course, is how to make good executives out of these candidates.

The task of selection can be broken down into several parts: (1) What are the best sources for sales executives; where should we go to find them? (2) What are the requirements of the job; what qualifications should we look for in our candidates? (3) Once we have found our candidates, how do we choose the best ones from among them?

The second task, that of making successful sales managers out of the best candidates, is one of choosing the right methods for developing aptitudes, habits, and skills which will lead to ultimate achievement.

It has sometimes been suggested that the same skills are required for sales executives that are prerequisite for general managers. Although many people may not agree with me, it has been my observation that more general executives are being chosen from the sales executive ranks than from other fields. Someone has advanced as a reason for this that sales managers acquire skill in handling exter-

NOTE: Mr. Tosdal is Professor of Business Administration, Harvard Business School; Mr. Stambaugh is Chairman of the Board, Standard Oil Company of Ohio; Mr. Cutright is Manager, Sales and Marketing Personnel Development, Marketing Services Division, General Electric Company; Mr. Olson is Partner, Booz, Allen & Hamilton; and Mr. Hansen is Professor of Business Administration, Harvard Business School.

Mr. Tosdal introduces the subject; Mr. Stambaugh and Mr. Cutright describe their company's practices and philosophies; Mr. Olson discusses the turnover problem; and Mr. Hansen brings in the viewpoint of salesmen and junior executives.

nal relations with people over whom they have no control; and this skill is an important function of top executives. But, even if true, does it follow that a general executive development program is appropriate for sales executives?

These — just by way of brief introduction — are some of the questions that we want to examine in the following pages. To do so, we shall look at the actual experience of some well-known companies.

Standard Oil Company of Ohio

The requirements for a sales manager will vary somewhat with the type of product sold and with the size of the company. Naturally the problems of the sales manager of a company that always sells its product to new customers — the one-time sale — are different from those of the one whose company sells over and over again to the same customers — who must live with his customers. Then, too, some sales managers are responsible only for actual sales, while others are in charge of warehousing, distribution, transportation, and servicing as well. Therefore, it is important to understand the background of a company and to have a knowledge of its policies and problems, before choosing its sales executives.

This is the story of Standard Oil of Ohio with which I am associated. Sohio sells gasoline, oil, and various products. Not only does it sell to independent retailers, but it also owns and operates 350 filling stations. The company stations offer the opportunity for merchandising experience, and the company regards them as incubators for management manpower. The company has both a "service" and a "sales" manager in one. It is a fairly large company, and the following discussion is necessarily in terms of the top echelon — the 40 or 50 top managers of the company.

The primary qualification for sales executives in Standard Oil is leadership — the ability to maximize the effectiveness of the organization by getting things done through the people under them. This qualification of course applies to all executives — not just sales executives. For purposes of analysis the sales executive's function can be divided into two separate areas — although of course these areas are really both part of the same job.

The first area is that of planning and administering the day-to-day operations for that part of his organization for which he is responsible. The other function — and it is one that is all too often overlooked by sales managers — is that of selecting, training, and developing executive power within his organization.

If I were looking for a sales executive, I would look for the man who puts the emphasis on the second area of sales executive management, that of training and developing men in his organization. I would even go further: I would be most delighted if I found a man who instinctively attempted to take care of the planning of a day-to-day sales organization by emphasizing entirely the matter of selecting, training, and developing his sales operation. In other words, I would be delighted to find a man who is equipped and inclined to build an organization and have it do the job — with the ideal, I suppose, that he himself had nothing to do with operations.

That never will happen — and of course it should not in just those terms. I am using extremes to make my point. As a matter of fact, I make a clear distinction between delegation and abdication, for I have no interest in the latter. It requires considerable talent to organize and delegate so that there is a clear understanding by all concerned of what has been delegated, and to whom, and how each should work with the others; and it requires also an ability to follow through with an awareness of how each man is carrying out the responsibility delegated to him. It takes far more talent to do this kind of job than it does to assign some task and walk away.

Therefore in looking for the ideal sales executive, I would look for one who organizes the job well and assigns it as a means of getting it done rather than for a man who instinctively attempts to centralize all the control in his own hands and consequently becomes a brake on the incentive of his men.

All my thoughts here imply decentralization of management. For if there is anyone who should be decentralized, it is the sales executive.

Now what are the traits, the qualities, and maybe the philosophies that we want to find in a man to make him, in our judgment, a good sales executive — a good leader? There are a lot of intangibles, and these may or may not be the ones that will do the job for each company, but I am sure that in almost every case some of them will enter into the qualifications of a good sales executive.

The first step that a good sales executive should take in starting his new job is to establish a working accord with his associates in top management. It follows therefore that the first test of whether or not he will do a good job is his ability to establish this accord easily and naturally. This is more than a communication of ideas; it is a community of spirit. A good leader instinctively tunes in on the wave length of his men, and they, in turn, acquire a feeling of confidence and understanding. Here are some of the intangible qualities that may lead to this accord:

(1) He should have a general love of people. I can hardly think of a sales executive who does not like people. If he is not an extrovert, he had better try to act like one.

(2) He ought to have the ability to command the respect of his men. He should stand for, culturally and morally, the things that they would admire.

(3) He ought to have the ability to put meaning into the job, to arouse the men's interest in the details of what they are doing, in contrast to his being only an emotional stem-winder. I cannot put too much stress on that point.

(4) He should have a spirit of dedication. He should love his job for its own sake. Of course, no sales manager can be expected to be indifferent to the salary attached to his job, but he himself and the job he does will both be much better if he enjoys his work and in that sense is dedicated to it. This test is high, but it is possible to find such men at all levels of an organization; so it is not impractical.

(5) He ought to have a realization that the organization rather than the leader is what counts. He must recognize that the achievement of others is one of his company's driving forces, too valuable to be dissipated in self-glory.

I get a little irked when I hear the head of an organization saying, "I did this," or "I did that." He did not do it in the first place, and it means he has forgotten one of the most important bases of sound leadership. I would like to have a man who realized that communication of ideas from the bottom to the top is often more important than the communication of ideas from the top to the bottom. The grass roots coming up to the top is the important thing, in large organizations especially.

(6) He should also have the appropriate intellectual equipment; we cannot overlook that. The intelligence test provides an indication of how far a man can rise in the organization, assuming other things are equal. However, intellectual ability is not enough. A sales executive has to deal with people; therefore he should be a man who understands people. The newsboy, the one who had to work his way through college, is more apt to have this ability instinctively than some of us who did not have the advantage of that background.

(7) He should have an objective and impersonal approach to any problem; this is one of the $64 qualities. And he cannot be too thin-skinned. Indeed he ought to welcome criticism; for he will get more help from the man who tries to take him apart than from all the "yes" men put together.

(8) He should be a man with good judgment; that is the test of sound sense, of both moral and practical values. In other words, he should be able to understand the significance of the experiences that he is having in his organization and to translate those experiences into policies.

(9) Finally, he should have good health. You can tell how far a frog will jump by his size. Health is a measure of a man's urge for power — how far he will go. I have made the mistake of allowing men who were ill to stay on the job because I liked them, but it was not fair to the rest of the company to do so. Good health in a sales executive is a vital part of his equipment, and I think we should insist upon it.

Now, after setting up the qualifications desirable for good sales executives, where do we turn to find potential candidates?

I feel that if we are not getting adequate sales managers through promotions from within, we ought to back up and put in some trainees. Wage rates should be high enough to attract men with the capacity to go to the top.

The job takes so much indoctrination — no company can function without a great deal of time spent on its problems, policies, and products — and if we have to go outside the company for a sales executive, we have to put him through a really prolonged course.

We have adopted such a trainee program. We have selected our men for ten years ahead, and we give them an extra course, extra rotation of experience, and extra pay. Opportunities for sales executive training are open to our present employees also.

I very strongly believe in building managers rather than buying them from the outside. The primary reason is that whereas all we can know about outside men is through secondhand recommendations, we have an opportunity for appraising our own trainees and our regular men. The only way I know of determining whether a man has character, integrity, and good judgment is by watching how he performs on different jobs.

General Electric Company

As was pointed out earlier, in order to understand the problem of choosing sales executives for a particular company, we must know something of the background of that company.

The General Electric Company organization is very much decentralized, as Mr. Cordiner explained in Part I of this book. We have 24 operating divisions and 101 operating departments — all with a high degree of autonomy. There are also 11 services divisions with responsibility for providing services, advice, and counsel to their particular executive officers, to the top group executives, and to other services divisions (as directed), and to operating divisions (as requested). These services divisions, in turn, include services departments.

Thus, the Marketing Services Division, the top marketing staff of the company, headed by the marketing vice president, includes the following services departments: (1) Sales — covering sales planning, sales management, and plain *selling* (I am old-fashioned enough to believe that word is significant) — and also (2) Marketing Research, (3) Product Planning, (4) Advertising and Sales Promotion, (5) Product Service, (6) Marketing Administrative Services, and (7) Marketing Personnel Development. (It is my function to manage both the Sales and the Marketing Personnel Development services departments.)

The General Electric concept of marketing differs somewhat from the old-fashioned sales manager idea. Each operating unit has a marketing manager, and he carries most of the responsibility for all aspects of marketing operations and is the focal point of decision. Under him are executives representing a division of labor in getting the goods to the market at the right place, at the right price, and at the right time, and of providing service after the sale. The sales manager, at the operating level, runs the field salesforce; the product planner works with the engineers to determine the kind of product we should sell; the advertising man handles advertising and promotion; the marketing administrative manager is responsible for finished goods and inventories, for warehousing, and for planning the production schedule for the factory; the marketing personnel development executive is responsible for selecting and training marketing management personnel; and so on — all counterparts of the top-level staff in the Marketing Services Division.

We in the Marketing Services Division act only in an advisory or consulting capacity so far as the operating units are concerned. Some of the operating divisions — for instance, the Lamp Division — run their own recruiting and training programs as they have every right to do, instead of making use of our Marketing Personnel Development Department which covers selection and training.

How does this organization influence our training program? It so happens that the problem of selecting and developing sales trainees varies somewhat according to product lines. In a large proportion of our units the engineering content is extremely heavy, and we cannot follow the same process that might be used by companies like Standard Brands or National Dairy. Our Apparatus Sales Division in Schenectady is in this category. Here engineers, assisted by men from the Marketing Services Division sales group, train men headed for Apparatus Sales. However, not until these trainees have taken the test course (an engineering training program) and worked in the product departments, is it decided definitely whether they will go into engineering or sales. (As a matter of fact, a certain portion of the men who finally get to be sales engineers come into the company by way of engineering selection.)

In the Marketing Services Division itself, we have a more advanced marketing training program. Our staff enters the picture when we bring in men from the graduate schools of business, such as Harvard, Columbia, Wharton, Michigan, or their equivalent. (We also locate some qualified men from inside the company who have had from three to five years' previous experience; we are always on the lookout for executive material.) We rotate this group through the seven functions previously mentioned, with actual case assignments on current "hot" problems. Men from different parts of our business direct these trainees in their field assignments, which run from six weeks to two months.

The functional breakdown, of course, leads to specialization; qualifications for one aspect of marketing may be out of place in another. Marketing research men are not always good salesmen, and product planning men are not always good marketing personnel development men. At the same time, some men are broad enough to develop. Job rotation, therefore, requires a balance between getting the benefits of specialization and broadening the background in the different functions.

After the training period is over, the men go into jobs on the operating level by selection and on a competitive basis. All we do is to indicate the kind of assignments that seem most in line with the capacities they have demonstrated during their training. Our instruction to the young man is, "You only have a job for the period of this training. After that your job is to get yourself sold at the operating level. The ultimate selection lies there."

We have recently started an advanced marketing management seminar for men slated for positions on a higher level. These men come to New York City for two weeks to study Harvard Business School cases in exactly the same way as is done in the Harvard AMP course, after which they return to their jobs for three weeks; then they come back to New York for a week, followed by two weeks on the job, and finally come back for one week again in New York — a total of four weeks. The group is small; for instance, 17 men are in the present course.

We also give special task force assignments to executives. For example, we have just completed a seven-month study of the marketing aspects of our producers' goods businesses, under my direction. It included nine senior marketing managers and three general managers. These men, during the life of the task force, served in the same way as would management consultants, rendering a report to the president and the executive vice presidents

Turnover of Sales Executives

Booz, Allen & Hamilton has recently published the results of a study on the subject of *The Growing Problem of Executive Turnover*. While this study does not deal specifically with the problem of sales executive turnover as a category, I have been asked to examine the underlying data for possible implications as to sales executives.

But, before I present my conclusions, I ought to give the major topics studied: (1) comparative turnover rates, prewar and postwar, (2) economic factors affecting executive turnover, (3) basic causes of separations, (4) why executives leave jobs, and (5) what can be done to reduce executive turnover.

Let me just run through the suggestions presented in connection with the fifth point, about reducing executive turnover, since they should have application to sales executives too:

(1) There should be a road map, or a long-range plan. Executives are more likely to stay with a company if they believe there is a plan for the business and, therefore, an opportunity for them.

(2) There should be a sound, flexible plan of organization in which executives can see opportunities for progress. Knowledge that such opportunities exist is essential for keeping men interested. Men will take all kinds of hardships if they have been warned in advance that meeting these hardships marks progress on the road to some goal.

(3) There should be a plan for selecting, training, and developing executives — a suggestion especially pertinent to our discussion here.

(4) There should be a modern plan of executive compensation — something that executives are somewhat interested in!

Now, let me get to my analysis of the underlying data. I have found some indication that there is a difference between turnover as applied to sales executives and other categories of executives; and I will cover the pertinent points even though the sample of sales executives, as a separate category, is thinner than it should be to draw firm conclusions.

With respect to all executives, postwar separations have been 29 per cent greater than prewar separations. This figure is based on a study of a specified number of jobs during the five prewar years and five postwar years. But in the case of sales executives, the percentage has been 17 per cent as compared with 29 — not nearly so great.

I am not sure that I can explain this difference, but I suspect that during the postwar period the pressure has not been on sales to anywhere near the degree it was in the prewar years; therefore, sales executives have been able to hold their jobs better than they did in that prewar pressure period. I would expect a greater increase in this figure for sales executives — it might even go beyond 29 per cent — if we move progressively into a buyers' market.

The next finding is that, of all executives leaving a company, 15 per cent separated at the company's initiative, that is, involuntarily. There is some question about the validity of this figure because of the difficulty of determining the real facts; there are times when separations appear to be resignations but are, in effect, at least *inspired* resignations. But the figure for sales executives should be significant for purposes of comparison. Only 11 per cent of sales executives left involuntarily.

Again, I think this lower figure reflects the position of business during the last five-year period in the economic cycle. Yet it may possibly be also an indication of the sales executive's ability to get along with people a little better than other executives. He may leave, but he does not leave so much because someone offered him more; he keeps his boss sold, so to speak.

In connection with the reasons given for separations, there also are some interesting, though slight, differences:

1. *Desire for diversified experience and broad background.* Of all executives on the move 8.1 per cent gave this reason for moving, compared with 12.9 per cent of the sales executives.

2. *Duties discontinued.* There was very little difference between the two groups.

3. *Location unsatisfactory.* Of all the executives about 6 per cent gave this as a reason, compared with 9.4 per cent of the sales executives.

4. *Anticipated sales merger or dissolution of the company.* Of all executives 4.5 per cent gave this as a reason, as compared with only 2.3 per cent of the sales executives.

5. *No challenge to the job.* Of all executives 4.3 per cent gave this reason, but only 3.5 per cent of the sales executives.

6. *Personality clashes.* Of all executives, 4.3 per cent gave this reason, but only 2.3 per cent of sales executives. Again this is an indication of sales executives' ability to get along without clashes.

These are the principal differences as gleaned from the data. They are interesting, but I do not feel that they are anything more than indications.

As I mentioned, one of of our proposed remedies for turnover is a plan for selecting, training, and developing executives. The following paragraphs from the publication are especially relevant:

An executive development program generally begins with an inventory of executive adequacy and potential, measured against a company's needs as revealed by a general survey of its organization, its current business, and its plans for the future. It progresses through selection of specific candidates and prospects for job openings, current and future, to planning the step-by-step development of individual executives. In its initial stages particularly, it frequently includes over-all training effort aimed at general improvement of the executive group.

The significant fact about executive development is that it has ceased to be a program. Once past its initial stages, executive development is a dynamic force acting on a manpower situation which changes almost daily and vitally affects every area of a company. Top executives have come to regard it and treat it as they do budgeting, something each line executive from the top down plans for and follows up continuously.

Executive development contributes most to controlling executive turnover by deliberately planning for it. The aims are to establish specifically what improvements in the management team are desirable, and to see that they take place as planned. Of necessity, the process involves planning for separations as well as for accessions of executive personnel . . .

It really hurts when an employee leaves after he has been selected and trained or developed — usually at considerable expense — to carry executive responsibility. This holds whether the executive leaves of his own accord or at the company's request. Either way, a costly error in planning or handling may have been made somewhere along the line. Executive development can work to assure that such errors occur as seldom as possible.

Viewpoint of Salesmen and Junior Executives

The brief observations that I am going to make may seem obvious, but sometimes it is extraordinarily difficult to see the obvious. I am simply going to report some of the things about executive development that have been told me by salesmen and junior-level executives.

(1) There is need for better job descriptions. Apparently the job descriptions many companies use have little to do with the way the company really operates. So it seems to me if we are going to develop sales executives, we must have more realistic job descriptions — not those idealistic affairs which say how things should be rather than the way they are.

(2) An inventory of usable individuals would be helpful. I have had men tell me that in very large corporations there is no inventory of their sales organization. One can always find somebody in the personnel department who can give information on how many people there are and how old they are, but information that would help in finding a usable individual just does not exist.

(3) More attention should be given to what the men who are being trained for executive positions think they need. It is a great temptation, certainly, to tell people what we think they need — "Here is a program all arranged" — but some firms have found it very useful to plan training programs with the participation of the men concerned. You can find out a lot if you get them to relax and tell you what is on their minds.

(4) Men all along the line should be trained to be as concerned with satisfying their subordinates as with pleasing their boss who is putting on the pressure. I am sure, despite all the talk we have about communication and its desirabilities, that more often than not people in organizations think more about satisfying the man above than satisfying the people below.

(5) There is need for better supervision. Some time ago a leading insurance company made a study of the turnover of its salesmen. One of the interesting conclusions that came out of the study

was that the reasons given for leaving the company did not differ significantly between the men who were successful in selling insurance and those who were unsuccessful. The real reason was that they simply did not have the kind of supervision they needed to get ahead. They had no one with whom they could talk over their problems, and they were dissatisfied.

(6) There should be more opportunity for change and travel. We talk a great deal of moving people from one district to another, of moving people from the line to the staff. But there are a lot of people in the sales organization who feel they are very definitely stuck somewhere out on the periphery. There may be opportunities at the home office, but the salesmen in the field do not see them.

(7) There should be more delegation of authority. In an organization where there is a great deal of sales pressure, people all down the line have the tendency to hold on to their responsibility to make sure the job gets done, whereas they would be more effective if they organized it and then assigned it to a subordinate.

HOW TO DEVELOP MANUFACTURING EXECUTIVES

Franklin E. Folts, Frank T. Lewis, and Ralph M. Hower

The most valuable single resource that a manufacturing company can have is a management team that works smoothly, that is organized to perpetuate itself along a steadily rising trend line of ability and capacity.

Most manufacturing resources are equally available in the market to all strong competitors. It is difficult to gain competitive advantage as to materials, labor, physical facilities, and even more difficult to hold any such relative advantage for any substantial length of time. However, no one can go into the market place and buy competent manufacturing management teamwork for spot delivery. Nor can anyone quickly and easily build such management teamwork, utilizing the resources at hand within the organization.

Thus, it follows that such a competent, resourceful management organization is well worth planning and working for, because once achieved it is a competitive advantage of enduring value. This is probably the most forceful argument for the placing of relatively high value on the smoothly operating management team as a manufacturing resource.

A strong, second argument for the constant development of management capacity is to be found in the nature of the manufacturing business.

It is trite, but true, that the one sure thing about tomorrow is that it will be unlike today. In this field, uncertainty and change are

NOTE: Mr. Folts is Professor of Industrial Management, Harvard Business School; Mr. Lewis is Manager, Manufacturing Personnel Development, Manufacturing Services Division, General Electric Company; and Mr. Hower is Professor of Business Administration, Harvard Business School.

Mr. Folts introduces the problem; Mr. Lewis considers it from the standpoint of the company; and Mr. Hower analyzes it from the standpoint of individuals being trained.

the only sureties. The single known means of meeting the demands of change in manufacturing is a management organization that is steadily growing as the result of constant self-development. In some competitive situations, this may even be an essential to survival.

From everyone's point of view, there are far too few competent manufacturing executives today. The common comment is, "If we could just lay our hands on a few really 'good' men, it would go a long, long way toward solving our problems."

Today's tax situation makes this business of finding and attracting competent, experienced executives much more difficult than it was a dozen years ago. It used to be that, other things being equal, an offer of a 20 per cent salary increase was substantial bait. I understand that to have any attraction for really desirable men, that figure now must be upped to some 40 or 50 per cent, and that even then it does not always shine.

The wide and rapidly growing interest in developing already available internal management resources and potentials is the natural result of this acute supply shortage and the impact of the adverse tax situation.

The internal development approach to the problem makes sense in several ways:

(1) Practically every manufacturing business of substantial size has within itself really adequate top-quality management potential. The problem is to spot this ability and to see that it grows.
(2) The most effective way to improve the rate of growth of experienced men of recognized ability is to make certain that they participate actively in the development of others.
(3) When carefully planned and carried out, company development of its own executive material usually is the least costly way of acquiring an outstanding management organization.

In other words, today's great interest in the development of managerial ability within a manufacturing company is no fad or fashion of the moment; rather, it seems to be a basic "must" in any program that proposes to achieve a superior competitive position.

The need for executive development in the manufacturing field is somewhat more important and acute than it is in some other fields of business. The reasons, I might say, are commonly recognized. The industrial superiority of this nation long has rested firmly on a foundation of technological ability and application.

At the same time, it is generally recognized, today, that this base is not broad enough. Thus, in the development of management skills in manufacturing, it becomes particularly important that we break with tradition and emphasize extending our knowledge and our know-how into the nontechnical areas of the factory; that we look at the people who work there, and their individual and group relationships, the problems of communication with them, and so on — look at them in a spirit of real understanding.

This need for breadth accounts, in part, for the great variety of the problems faced by those who have the responsibility for executive development. The following are characteristic problems:

Who should be responsible for executive development in this field? Should it be all executives and all supervisors — everyone who has any administrative or executive responsibility — or should the responsibility for development and training rest with a specialist group; or should the responsibility rest with the individual who seeks to better himself, who wants promotion, who possesses the all-important drive to succeed?

Who should be developed and trained? Should it be everyone, or selected individuals? How does one select? How extensive a program will it be? How far up the executive scale should it go? Or, how far down the executive scale should it go?

Which produces the better results — the formal training program or the informal method of coaching? Then, too, how can results be judged? Who should appraise the progress, and how?

Above all, how can we get the new values that we are after, and yet at the same time make certain that we do not sacrifice those values that we already possess?

Clearly, the range of questions is well beyond our capacity to dispose of in this chapter, but at least we can look at what are probably the more basic aspects of the over-all problem.

General Electric Company

Training men for responsibility and leadership in manufacturing has been an important industry function for many years, but recent trends and new techniques, including the "push-button" or "automatic factory," emphasize the importance of developing outstanding talent in this field. Surveys of manpower requirements in the areas of supervision, manufacturing engineering, production planning, purchasing, and so on, point up the magnitude of the job that lies ahead.

New products can no longer be introduced into our shops without undergoing several stages of preliminary planning by the manufacturing organization, starting when the product is in the early stages of design. This approach calls for high-grade manufacturing or industrial engineers and production and materials analysts, in addition to the usual manufacturing supervision. Only when a group of such men work closely with the design engineers, marketing, and financial men do we obtain the best over-all operating results.

Selection and training cannot be a haphazard affair. Rather they must be organized and carefully administered. Furthermore they must be conducted at a level which will replace and supplement the organization as the needs arise.

Assuming that we have a reasonably adequate supply of well-educated young men from our technical schools and colleges — and at the same time recognizing that no two individuals are ever alike — we are faced with the problem of orientation and on-the-job training during their early years in industry. We must have programs that hold the trainee's attention and challenge his ability, in order to supplement properly the previous academic work. Moreover, the program must be flexible enough to meet the individual needs of young men who have a wide variety of aptitudes, education, and general background.

There are several phases of manufacturing training that I should like to discuss. It seems to me that the best way to bring out the important points is to present them in the form of questions and answers which will serve to explain this activity in the General Electric Company. The main questions are:

1. What constitutes a comprehensive manufacturing manpower development program?

2. Assuming that the available candidates have good educational backgrounds in technical and administrative fields, what kind of men do we want for our factory organizations?

3. Where do they come from?

4. How many training levels are necessary for the development and progress of outstanding men?

With reference to the first question, we have found in our company that it is important to train at all levels, starting with *apprentices* in the trades, such as machinists, tool and die makers, draftsmen and tool designers, patternmakers and foundrymen.

Our next level is that of *manufacturing specialists,* who are given special training in such areas as methods and plant layouts, planning and wage rates, production control, motion-time analysis, and quality control.

The next level, *supervision and foreman training,* is probably the most important of all. It is here that labor meets management, and it is of the utmost importance that we continue to do a better administrative job and establish better communications with our first-line supervision. These men are given special courses in employee relations, union contracts, safety and housekeeping, quality control, service to customers, expense and cost control, spoilage and waste, direct labor control, and so forth.

Manufacturing engineering and *manufacturing management* represent the next level of training. This, when combined with our courses of evening study — 2 hours per session, 2 sessions per week, 36 weeks per year, for 3 years — is equivalent to graduate work in engineering or business administration. Whereas the lower level programs are given in the local plants, from this point on the training is conducted on a company-wide basis.

Our next and final level, of any formal nature, is that of *department and division management training,* in which the older men are given relatively long intrafunctional and interfunctional assignments in one or more of our operating departments.

Thus, it is through a series of training opportunities that our most outstanding men can receive adequate training at any level for which they are qualified.

The second question, concerning the kind of men we desire for our factory organizations, can be answered briefly. There are two types: (a) the leader and supervisory type, and (b) the specialist and analytical type. In this present period of industrial expansion, we need both types, and it is most difficult to decide which of the two is more important.

As for the third question, concerning where they come from, we draw on a variety of sources. A surprising number of men without any formal education whatever are able to join our programs and compete successfully; hence, many men qualify from our operating areas, that is, men who were hired directly from the street. Also our apprentice programs supply a large percentage of the manufacturing specialists and foremen; and many of these men go on to even higher levels.

Promotion takes place out of all levels of supervision. Candidates for our three-year manufacturing training program are recruited from the other company programs, as well as from colleges and engineering schools; and from here the men go directly into manufacturing training at the department or company level.

This leads to a question that is often asked, as to whether we prefer for our manufacturing training program the boy directly from college or the man who has come up through the shops. About 40 per cent of the candidates in this program are from the shops. There are always some men with no formal education, some who are outstanding graduates of our apprentice schools, and some with four or five years of shop experience and several years of college, technical school, or business school. Actually, we have found very little difference in their performance.

The important thing is that we get men with a high degree of mechanical aptitude and leadership, quite apart from their formal education. Of course, the formal education is all to the good; and if we look for that too, we are likely to get better men. But it is quite surprising to find the latent talent that we have throughout our shops; in all parts of the company there are men coming in at the lowest level and going right straight through to the top. I would say that we need both types of men, and that we have yet to find out just what the right mixture is.

Finally, as to the fourth question, concerning the number of training levels that are necessary for the development and the progress of outstanding men, I would say that the pattern varies from a few to many. Our policy is to make a very thorough analysis of each individual's background and training. We carefully explore his indicated aptitudes and observe him closely during the first year. Only then are we able to plan the proper course of study and training for the individual with respect to his indicated potential.

In connection with planning a course of study and training for an individual I have been asked about the use of tests for screening prospective management trainees.

I honestly think that we are taking a realistic approach to this question. Aptitude tests were developed at the General Electric Company some 25 years ago. They are practical, down-to-earth tests and are given to new applicants to determine aptitudes such as finger dexterity; and there they serve to minimize a great deal of turnover in our attempts to find the best type of people to go on delicate assembly operations and work of that sort. We have also used tests to a certain extent in determining clerical aptitudes.

More recently, we have become interested in tests for selecting potential management material and for determining the aptitudes and personality traits of executive candidates up through to the higher levels. We make good use of tests of this kind after the trainees are recruited from colleges, but only to a slight extent in our recruiting from our ranks. We need it in the case of the colleges. There is such a mad scramble on the college campuses today that we rarely have over 20 minutes to talk to a boy, and it is very difficult to learn very much about him in such a short time. So, as a supplement to the interview, we give him a battery of tests—not as a condition of employment, but as a straw-in-the-wind, and as a guide to our future counseling of that man.

While I am on this subject, I should also mention a simple device that we are using. We build a profile of each candidate whom we bring into our manufacturing training program. Here we take three sets of criteria into account: (1) We have three or four indices of academic achievement. (2) We have an evaluation of the man's practical experience, if any. (3) We have three or four more indices based on tests. From all these, we plot a vertical line that veers from left to right indicating the man's strengths and weaknesses.

Let us say that a man has been with us, and we have had an opportunity to observe him, for two or three months. Then we sit down with him and review the chart. We compliment him for his achievements and then tell him of places where we would like to help him. This approach has been very effective.

Every once in a while, there is an occasion where a test will bring out something that is helpful, but usually it does not show us much more than we already know, particularly about the men who have been with us for a year or two. We never go into any of the really negative aspects of a test, but we suggest that the man ought to concentrate on this or that element and arrange with the instructors for him to take the necessary courses. And then, maybe six months later, we talk to the man again.

In getting acquainted with a trainee and evaluating his performance, I do not think that there is anything that beats a series of multiple interviews.

One basic principle that we have in our manufacturing training program is that every participant, no matter what he is going to become finally, should get anywhere from three to six months' experience of actual floor supervision. We plan to give him at least one assignment where he has to handle some 30 or 40 people, answering the everyday, common, run-of-the-mill questions from the productive operators, both men and women. This is one of the most valuable training spots that we know about. In fact, it is the place where one kind of people can be divided from the other. We have found that the fellow who likes to work with people is the fellow who shines in this kind of assignment.

In order to be prepared for this supervisory assignment, the trainee must have been rotated through various spots on the lower level of operations. Then he can say, as he goes along, that he has been there, that he has handled that sort of thing; and if the people whom he is called on to supervise know him, it is of tremendous help to him.

I have experienced that same thing in the shops myself. I grew up in the shops; I worked there for almost 30 years. In my earliest days I was an apprentice toolmaker. This experience has always been of great value to me, in sitting down and talking with people about planning and design of tools and equipment, because the ones I happened to be associated with knew that I had been "through the mill."

The practice of moving people up through these several levels is very important, especially in the lower levels of supervision. Indeed, it is often dangerous, particularly in the case of certain individuals, to try to skip some of these levels. Such experience is essential if the program is not to be theoretical and abstract.

This is a brief outline of some of the many things that we are doing, and the things that we believe must be done, if we are to have a sufficient number of well-trained men during the period ahead.

The period outlined here covers approximately 10 years of a man's industrial life; and, even then, that is not the end of training and development for the man who continues to go up the ladder.

While my outline may have appeared very formal, as a matter of fact it represents a very practical, down-to-earth training on the job. We believe wholeheartedly in training on the job. We believe in thus exposing our trainees to opportunities where they gain experience by association with others.

In sum, it is the continuous concern of our personnel people to watch for talent, and, through appropriate training and job opportunities, to make sure by means of a careful appraisal that the individual is placed on work best suited to his personality, and in which he can be most effective as a leader or as a specialist in the operations of one of the units of our company.

Finally, let me emphasize that there is one thing that is essential in training, particularly in a large organization like the General

Electric Company, and that is acceptance of the idea from top management on down that there is a movement through an organization, that there are bound to be young men coming in one way or another, and that, rather than have this movement a haphazard affair, there should be some order to it.

The Employees' Viewpoint

I am going to try to look at this question of developing manufacturing executives in a very elementary kind of way. So often, today, when we talk about executive development or training programs, we are thinking in terms of formal training efforts on an organized basis. In that concept there is a danger that we shall lose sight of a related although different idea: that men on the job are always learning from their supervisors and from the people around them, even though there isn't any training program as such. In other words, every supervisor, every man in a position of superiority over others, whether he is aware of it or not, is exerting an educational influence. And quite frequently the educational message which is being conveyed by the behavior of the supervisor is at some variance with the formal message that the supervisor and the management in general would like to have conveyed.

Here is what happens to the man on the job — say, a foreman with several years' experience. An executive in the company, who has read in the *Harvard Business Review* or *Fortune* or somewhere that training programs are good things, gets a program organized to give this man and his fellow foreman some know-how in management. The program is likely to include some technical information on methods work, time study, production control, and so on. Then there may also be some principles of general management — delegating responsibility and authority, encouraging participation in department problems, and so on.

What is being taught the man through the formal program, however, too often does not match what is being taught to him in the everyday relationships on the job. Sometimes, the very supervisor who tells him that he must delegate responsibility and give his subordinates a chance to figure out some answers and make some decisions is violating those rules constantly.

In such circumstances, which aspect of the educational process is likely to be more influential, which one is the fellow really going to observe? I believe a man will learn more from the day-to-day behavior of his superior, not only because there is more of it, time-wise, but also because there are management pressures — qualifications for promotion, approval of one's supervisor, and that sort of thing — which tend to make the man believe it essential for him to conform to the behavior and examples he sees.

Even if the organized program is an intensive one — an evening a week for a period of three months or three weeks full-time, or whatever it may be — it is likely to have less relative impact than the day-to-day influences which are in opposition to it.

Now, it seems to me that, following from our look at the job of training in this way, there are some specific questions that we ought to be asking ourselves:

(1) What is the man really learning — as distinct from what he is being "taught"? One can find out easily enough what people are consciously and articulately teaching. But what is being learned, from the behavior of people, is harder to determine.

(2) Do we like what he is learning — that is, is it in accordance with our ideas of developing executives for manufacturing, or is it at variance with what we want? It may be, as I have suggested, in conflict with the very things that we have set as our objectives.

(3) If the training that is being given by supervisory behavior is not what we want, what do we do about it? How do we manage to bring about a situation in which men will be learning the kind of things we think they need in order to be prepared to assume the responsibilities of manufacturing executives? There is more to it than simply deciding on the material to be covered and then organizing a course to teach it. This does not mean that formal training programs are a mistake; or that we should not formulate objectives and procedures and set up a series of courses to train men for executive positions in the field of manufacturing. All that I am trying to suggest is that we take a good look at the situation that lies in front of us, and then adapt our program to what we find.

All this may sound very simple and straightforward, but it is difficult to carry out. Employees are apt to be reluctant to report that what is being taught to them formally is quite different from what the boss actually does, for it means that the boss does not do what he is supposed to do. The boss might not appreciate things like that being said about him, even though the other things reported about him at the same time were good.

The only solution is to get in and observe what is going on; to become acquainted, on an easy and friendly basis, with the trainees; to listen with very sensitive ears and try to pick up the messages that are usually floating around.

There is always the problem, also, of how to find the men who are really interested in being trained for more responsible jobs. Training programs are all too often based on the premise that since all men *should* be interested in getting ahead, all men *are* interested in getting ahead; and consequently the problem of motivation is not even tackled.

This, of course, is unrealistic. It is very difficult to drive people through training programs, and it is foolish to expect very significant results from people who are so driven. I suspect that we could save a good deal of money by trying to find out, first, what kind of training men are interested in and, secondly, in what areas of their work they feel need for help.

This, again, means a kind of individual survey of the situation, because different men need different things. One of the points I wish to make here is that even a small business, which is not in the position to contemplate an elaborate, formal program or series of programs, may offer opportunities for men to learn more than they are learning now. The task is for someone to put his mind to discovering where these opportunities exist.

Another aspect of our problem of developing executives is the question of who should conduct the training program. In a company large enough to have a staff or a service organization, it seems to me that the training is likely to be somewhat better executed if it is placed in the hands of people who have some special interest in training and have had preparation for that job. Just as there are people who are very good at supervision but are not interested in the educational aspects of a job and have no particular talent for it, so there are people who are good at teaching a job but who may have serious weaknesses as supervisors. If you have an organization large enough to place special talents in nice compartments, it is a better use of your resources to have a staff training group made up of such people.

But what are the line-staff relationships in such a case? It seems to me on that question there can be no quibbling. The authority must be the line supervisor's; I do not see that his life can be very tolerable if he does not have the final say.

This may sometimes be a little difficult for the staff people to accept because they feel quite strongly that they ought to get the supervisor to do certain things and that he hasn't sense enough to do it without being pushed. On the other hand, the training people can be very helpful to the line people if their attitude is somewhat as follows: "We are equipped to do some training when you want some help. We think that we can be of service, but we are not going to force our services upon you. If you want help, don't hesitate to let us know, and we will try to work out with you a program which fits the needs of your particular situation, as you see it."

This is an offer of help and not a threat of interference. Therefore it is more likely to be accepted and taken advantage of. The start may be a little slow, but once a staff organization does get going on that basis, the line people are pretty apt to come around begging for help.

But what about the organization that is too small to have much in the way of staff or service personnel? It seems to me that whether you have a staff training section or not, the line supervisors ought always to be thinking in terms of: "How can I help these people do a better job? What help do they need?"

And, if a man is really concerning himself about that, it seems to me that he is likely to be talking with his subordinates and saying: "Are you running into any problems where you need some help? If so, don't hesitate to ask me about it, because I will try to help you if I can. We will get some help for you." So it comes back to the basic attitude of trying to help someone do his job, trying to help him get ahead and learn more things, but placing upon him the responsibility for saying when he needs help and what kind of help he needs.

But how can the weak supervisor be made to realize the necessity for self-improvement without destroying his morale? The answer will vary according to the situation.

Many companies have a regular performance review of some sort at frequent intervals. If this review is carried out thoroughly, the man knows wherein he is deficient, and it is up to him to do something about it. At the same time, he knows that other people are going through the same process, and it is a little easier for him to take suggestions.

If there is no regular performance review of this kind, the problem is more difficult. One way which I do *not* recommend is for his superior to say to him, in essence: "You know, Joe, that you're not doing a very good job here, and you have got to improve, or else!" He is apt to reply: "I'm going to improve and be better — but, to get down to specifics, improve in what way?"

Suppose the explanation is: "You must do a better job of administering discipline," or "You have to do a better job of getting the work done at close tolerances," or whatever it may be. Then the fellow might say: "You know, that's right; I've got to do a better job on that." And there it stops; nothing constructive is achieved.

A slightly different approach is to say to the man: "There is something that I think you ought to know. We have observed places where your performance can be strengthened." There is no beating around the bush here — none of that indirect, so-called diplomatic approach which either does not fool anybody or fails to convey any information. But the emphasis is not on the weaknesses as such; rather it is on points where the performance could be strengthened — with help.

One of the tests of the man with executive potential is the desire to get ahead, a sense of personal responsibility for his own development. If we drive him, we do not know whether he has that power within him or not. But suppose we put upon his shoulders the responsibility for saying: "I do want to get ahead. I do want to learn these things, and here is the kind of help that I would like to get." If we get him to say that, then it seems to me that we are helping that man to develop self-reliance, which is quite important.

In conclusion, the problem of developing men for more responsible positions calls for us to start thinking in terms of what we can do for the individual: Who is he, how are we going to teach him, what is it that we want him to be taught, what is it that he needs to be taught, what is it that he wants to be taught? But, paradoxically, we want him to think about these matters too, and to participate in formulating the answers. As I see it, we must avoid doing his thinking for him.

In the last analysis, all we can do is to offer opportunities, and the opportunities which will be most attractive are those which fit a man's needs, as he sees them.

HOW TO DEVELOP CONTROLLERS

Thornton F. Bradshaw, A. O. Savage, Fritz J. Roethlisberger, and Russell H. Hassler

Recently I was talking with a company president about developing men for a controllership, and he said: "Why bother? Why not concentrate your efforts on developing executives?" That seems to me a significant observation and one that is representative of the new and growing concept of controllership. Let me explain what I mean in more specific terms:

Several months ago I was in a southern plant of a large company. On the staff of the plant manager is a cost and planning man who reports directly to the plant manager. He is responsible for the operation of the standard cost setup, for studies of machinery replacement, for helping the production people set goals, for keeping the plant manager informed as to the progress toward those goals, and so on; in other words, he is the plant manager's analytical right-hand man. Also on the staff of the plant manager there is a plant controller who reports functionally to the main office controller. He is responsible for the books of account, the payables and receivables, the payroll, and the inventory records.

It seems clear, in such a setup, that the one man is rapidly going up toward the ranks of top management and the other is remaining static or even going down.

This illustrates what has happened to the whole concept of controllership. Within the ranks of controllers, there has been a very large and noticeable split. One group is moving rapidly toward

NOTE: Mr. Bradshaw is a Principal in the firm of Cresap, McCormick and Paget; Mr. Savage is Assistant Comptroller, Standard Oil Company of New Jersey; Mr. Roethlisberger is Wallace Brett Donham Professor of Human Relations, Harvard Business School; and Mr. Hassler is Professor of Accounting, Harvard Business School.

Mr. Bradshaw is responsible for the introduction; Mr. Savage describes philosophy and practice in his company; Mr. Roethlisberger discusses the human relations aspects; and Mr. Hassler contributes the concluding observations.

top management; many of them have attained that position. The other group is not merely remaining static; it is actually moving away from a position in top management, becoming more specialized, more outside the management process.

How has this change come about? My own theory is that it stems from two things which have happened to management in the last 20 years: (1) Profits no longer constitute a sufficient standard for making decisions within the large corporation or within the medium-size corporation. (2) The job of president has become far too big for any one man. Let us look at these two propositions a little more closely.

Consider the sales manager of the typical large company. What is the standard by which he makes his decisions — if left alone? His objective may be to increase sales each year. Perhaps his objective is to blanket the country with his products. The accomplishment of these goals may or may not add to profits, may or may not contribute to the attaining of a profit objective. Standing by themselves, there is no reason why they should.

Look at the production manager. What is his objective? It may be to utilize his machinery to full capacity or to tool each part to the full capability of the machine. Or it may be to arrive at the lowest possible scrap loss. It is always possible to attain a low scrap loss — by paying a high price in slowdown of production, which in turn means compromising profits.

Look at the credit manager. If left alone, his objective is to reduce credit losses to an absolute minimum. There is one way to do that — to refuse all sales on which there is any kind of risk.

I hesitate to raise the question of the objectives of the research director — we must make sure that the dignity of research is maintained — but it is common knowledge that they can be quite nebulous.

In a large corporation, each department is a pressure group with its own objectives in mind. As in any such situation, when the pressure group goes to work, it goes to work for its own objectives. And if it attains all of its objectives, it probably does so at the cost of the other groups.

So it has come about that the profit standard, by which the owner-manager of a small business makes his decisions and is quickly and effectively judged, does not exist in the functional departments of today's large companies — unless it is *created*.

There is, of course, one man who has the profit standard in mind in making decisions, and who is judged by the over-all profit attained by the company. That man is the president. Take the situation — familiar to all of us — where the officers are gathered to discuss the capital budget. The research director wants a big program because he has the future in the palm of his hand; the production manager wants a new plant so he can turn out more units faster; and the sales manager wants a foreign subsidiary so he can travel over to Paris twice a year. Who is going to decide among these competing interests? The president must decide, but he cannot decide wisely on the basis of just listening to these pressure groups. To help him decide he needs planned objectives for each department, which taken together will result in the attainment of a planned company goal.

This leads us to the second point — that the job of president is too big for any one man. What is the job of president? He has to set a profit goal for the company to attain. He has to set standards of performance for each department so that those standards, taken together, will attain that profit goal. He has to set up a method of following the progress of each department toward that goal. And, finally, he has to make adjustments to make sure that the whole organization is running smoothly and that the over-all objective is attained in harmony. Certainly the job of president — even when expressed in these simplified terms — is far too big for any one man.

On whom can the president call for help in developing the standards for the various departments, which when taken together will achieve the planned profit goal? There have been instances where he has called on the controller — cases where the controller was already moving in the direction of meeting top management's needs. But in other instances, where the controller was moving toward expertness in tax affairs or refinement of the cost system, the president has reached out and knighted someone else. The reader has noted, I am sure, the number of new titles which have appeared on the corporate scene: Vice President in Charge of Control, Vice President in Charge of Planning, Vice President in Charge of Coördination.

There is more than a matter of definition involved here. We are dealing with two distinct functions, and one man probably cannot do both of them. In some organizations — for instance, Ford and U. S. Steel — both kinds of work are handled by the same department; but, significantly, the departmental organization is split right down the line vertically. On one side are the people who keep the records and handle the payroll, the tax people, and the other specialists. On the other side are the analysts, the people who stand behind the man at the open hearth and the people who stand behind the president and help him make decisions, help him coördinate the whole business.

Such an organization can be successful; but, if so, it is because the man who heads it is a good administrator. But the cleavage is still there. This inevitable split in functions poses the crucial question in this matter of developing men for controllership: Developing them for what?

If we are developing them for expertness, for the group that I believe is moving away from top management, then we have one kind of problem — and not a very difficult problem. Our schools are geared for producing technicians and our companies, by the natural working of executive advancement, produce technicians quite normally.

If, on the other hand, our objective is one of an entirely different nature — creating men for what is really a new function, this idea of "expanded presidency" — then the problem of developing men is difficult. We have to face up to the fact that many of our schools, business schools particularly, are geared to produce technicians. There are very few schools which realize that more is going to be wanted of these men than competence in specialized techniques.

But scholastic background is only part of the problem. Equally significant is the way companies develop or fail to develop executives. What so often happens in the natural course of business is that companies take specialists from the schools, refine them and make bigger technicians out of them. After a man has spent years learning to handle the detail of his specialty — accounting, for instance — he is required to become a generalist in order to meet management's needs for planning and control. Small wonder that so many fail.

On the other hand, some forward-looking companies are preparing men with the new controllership in view. But I am not going to discuss what a company can do in this area, for that is the subject of the following section.

Standard Oil Company of New Jersey

Jersey Standard has a stock ownership of 50 per cent or more in 213 companies, employing approximately 147,000 people. These companies are engaged in all phases of the petroleum business. They operate in 130 different countries and conduct business in many languages and, of course, in many currencies. As a shareholder in all these affiliated companies, Jersey holds them responsible for the efficient operation of their respective organizations. It is for this reason that it is particularly important for Jersey to assure itself constantly that each affiliate does have a good management and that there will be continuity of competent management.

This is mentioned to point up the obvious necessity of entrusting wide authority and responsibility to the managements of these affiliates. Each single one of them, whether wholly-owned or not, has its own board of directors, responsible to all its shareholders (including Jersey) for its actions and for the success of its operations. Experience has shown that such far-flung operations cannot be conducted efficiently on any other basis. Foremost among the benefits derived from this high degree of decentralization is the development of people — their initiative, their leadership, and their resourcefulness.

Under such circumstances, the controllership responsibilities are heavy. The controller of each affiliate scattered around the world reports administratively to his own local management, but he does have certain functional responsibilities to the controller of the Jersey parent company. And among the duties of the Jersey parent controller and his staff is the responsibility to counsel with the Jersey board on the question of affiliated company controllers and their staffs — a large order that must be worked at day in and day out.

In the office of the parent-company controller, we perform an advisory service, rather than setting up definitive procedures for the affiliate company controllers to follow. We do issue an accounting manual which covers the financial statement requirements for preparing stockholder reports and reports to the Securities Exchange Commission; that is a necessity. And we do make suggestions about cost accounting procedures, but they are always subject to changes and ideas proposed by the accountants of the affiliated companies. And when our internal auditors, or the independent public accountants, run into a method or system that is not sound, we of course offer our suggestions. But that is about as far as we go in that area.

Our main function is one of appraisal. And here we try to be quite thorough. Prompt receipt by the Jersey controller of properly prepared financial and cost statements is not necessarily a safe criterion in itself that an affiliated company is staffed with good management in the controller's department. In addition we must know the people involved and know them well; and we must form an opinion as to the quality of each staff's performance — both its weaknesses and strengths.

We try to accomplish these understandings and evaluations in many ways — personal visits to the affiliates; accounting conferences that are attended by representatives of the affiliates; audit reports, both from the internal auditors and the independent public accountants; scheduled visits to our office in New York, of a training nature, for the representatives of the affiliated companies; and so on.

Perhaps more significant, what factors do we consider in evaluating the job being performed? Of course, there are many, many factors involved: the dollar cost of the job being done, service to local management, the adequacy of the internal controls, proper financial reporting, and so forth. But paramount is the administrative ability of the controller himself.

Accordingly, we consider it significant to know whether the affiliated-company controller has a sound organizational structure, and whether he is selecting, training, and promoting strong people. This matter of selection and training is important because our affiliates provide career employment, and selecting the wrong people can be a very serious mistake as far as the organization is concerned and as far as the people involved are concerned. Under Jersey policy of promotion from within, we cannot have strong men at the top unless we bring in men with high potentials at the bottom.

We believe that there is need to give every individual an opportunity to utilize his ability to the maximum, and there is also responsibility not only to see that the day-to-day work is done efficiently but also that it is done in an atmosphere of congeniality and contentment. So we inquire as to what the controller's relations are in the organization, both vertically and horizontally. We ask ourselves if they are good or bad, and why. We ask, too, whether the controller has a program for periodically evaluating people; and, if so, whether he combines it with personal counseling, in order to help his people overcome their weaknesses and to help them develop their strengths.

Particularly important, does the controller delegate responsibility and authority to his subordinates? The significance of this question is that such delegation results (a) in a better job being done day to day both in the sense of greater output capacity on the part of the controller's department and (b) in the sense of greater feeling of participation on the part of subordinates. Training men to think and act responsibly is a key to the development of a succession of able administrators and hence continuity of competent management; it is one of the most crucial aspects of the whole problem of developing men for controllership.

Even though a controller may be unusually well endowed with intelligence and technical competence, any strong tendency on his part to use these faculties for doing things himself, for getting bogged down in technicalities rather than for selecting good technicians, getting the work done through them, and then sizing up and taking the results to top management, will most certainly cause a serious decline in the effectiveness of his entire staff and in his own fall from the top management team where he belongs.

We encourage the controller to keep his subordinates well informed and to confer with them on the formulation and execution of plans. As I mentioned earlier, the development of strong, broad-gauged controllers is primarily the responsibility of affiliated companies, with the parent-company controller acting only in an advisory capacity.

This job, we feel, cannot be left to chance. It must begin with the selection of individuals with high potential capacity, followed by periodic evaluations and personal counseling.

No matter how carefully selected, they will have weaknesses as well as strengths. Hence there must be periodic evaluations to determine what each individual has and what he needs. For example, he may need training in certain operating phases of the business, or he may need development in the operation of an effective department, or he may need further professional training, or he may need to minimize some undesirable personal characteristics. In these evaluations, the rating is done by the individual's supervisors. The head of the division, the man's immediate supervisor, and any supervisors in between independently fill in a regular rating form, then get together and discuss him; and, once there is a meeting of the minds concerning him, the immediate supervisor goes over the appraisal with him and makes suggestions for improvement. Note that the same supervisor does the counseling, not someone from the industrial relations department as in some companies.

In this evaluation and counseling we feel we have an effective procedure, not only for helping the man overcome his weaknesses and develop his strengths, but also for keeping him from getting lost in the organization as a technician when actually he has the capacity for going on to greater responsibilities. There may be 150 or 200 people in the controller's department, as well as 14 or 15 division heads and 30 or 40 intermediate supervisors. So it is important for both the individual and the company that there be a procedure like this for picking out the best man, filling in the gaps in his background, and training him for better things.

We feel that it is as important to tailor our training to each individual's needs as it is for a doctor to determine medication only after careful diagnosis of a particular patient's ills. The blanket or fixed type of training for all individuals is likely to accomplish very little and be expensive besides.

Now, this tailored training that I am referring to might consist of any one or more of the following assignments in our organization: opportunities to observe various phases of operations, including physical aspects of exploration for oil, crude oil production, pipeline and marine transportation, refining, and marketing; rotation training assignments, both within the controller's department and outside; committee assignments; assignments of increasing responsibilities; moving trainee around to get appraisals from other administrators; personal consultation; and, of course, academic training in accounting, public speaking, and so on; and special programs offered by some of the university graduate schools for men who have had substantial business experience at the management level.

The affiliates of course have responsibility for selecting and training their own men. We in the parent office work with them in an advisory capacity. When we make our visits, we inquire about their programs for building replacements of older personnel, for going out to colleges and selecting good men — how they go about it, what interviewing and other techniques they use — and of course for orienting, rating, counseling, and training the men they do hire. Also we will sometimes help them find a man for a particular spot, since naturally we often know of men in other affiliates who would be suitable.

Back home at the parent company we try to practice what we are preaching. We go to the universities to hire what we hope are good men. We take them in numbers large enough to take care of our normal losses annually through attrition, retirement, death, and so on; and we feed them in through the bottom always. Then we start our process of development.

We have one training program which is four and a half years in length. We take promising young men; send them to operating affiliates (foreign or domestic) where they observe exploration, production, refining, transportation, marketing activities, and related accounting. They write reports and study as they go along. Some of those young men will just notice the flow of paper and the mechanical things. Others are broad enough to recognize good organization when they see it; bad practices when they see them; what makes one office run better than another; and the like. We move these men along, always evaluating and counseling and tailoring any further training to their individual needs; and maybe sooner or later they are ready to fill administrative jobs.

In sum, the successful development of controllers, as well as the coördination of other activities in the Jersey family, is a widespread coöperative effort among the affiliates and the parent company. We strive for group decisions as far is is practicable, in preference to decisions by a single individual, however wise he might be.

Human Relations

I am assuming that my assignment is to share my ignorance with others. What I know about the technical activities of controllers is practically zero. About the consequences of their behavior for other people in the organization, however, I have heard a great deal. Therefore, I shall attempt to develop this point. I believe it has a close bearing on our theme, "How to develop controllers."

According to theory, the purpose of the controller is to serve the people in line management by providing them with information that will allow them to do a better job. This being so, how does it so often happen that the people in the controller's office are regarded by the people in the line management (particularly those at lower levels) as a source of interference rather than as a source of help? This is the question I should like to consider.[1]

[1] In preparing this statement I have borrowed very freely from the findings of Chris Argyris, *The Impact of Budgets on People,* prepared for the Controllership Foundation, Inc., by The School of Business and Public Administration, Cornell University.

Let me start by looking briefly first at the way controllers view their activities and then at how factory supervisors view these same activities.

Quite properly controllers believe that they serve very important functions. They constitute "the eyes and ears of the plant." They provide those figures which set the goals of the organization. They also provide those figures which show whether or not the goals have been met. In terms of these variances between actual and standard, they keep line management informed about where it stands. As controllers see it, these figures not only furnish a goal but also a challenge to factory people. They are the vehicle for improvement and change, for increased productivity and efficiency. Inconsistencies, errors, and weaknesses can be quickly located; improvements can be quickly made. As a result, factory people are "kept on their toes" and are motivated to do a better job.

Most controllers are aware that their outlook on these matters is not shared by the operating people. But this difference they explain by saying that factory supervisors tend to look at things from the short-run rather than from the long-run point of view. Unlike them, operating people have not been trained to think logically and analytically and to see things objectively and as they are. Hence controllers perceive their problems with operating people as being due to lack of education, lack of information, or lack of understanding about what controllers are up to. Their solution, therefore, runs in the direction of educating and training factory supervisors with regard to the use and need of cost standards, how these standards are constructed, and so on.

Now let us look at the same activities from the point of view of shop supervisors. How do they talk and feel and think about these same activities? They find that these figures which controllers provide, far from presenting the "cold pictures" of why things are the way they are, show them instead why things are not the way they have been or should be. To them this is a "horse of a different color." Such pictures are fraught with emotion and feeling. They can arouse — and more often than not do arouse — fear, resentment, hostility, and aggression instead of encouragement, stimulation, and good cheer.

To the factory supervisor the living and important reality is today — not yesterday or tomorrow. With the controller's emphasis on past and/or future performance, he ignores the present. But, to boot, he uses the past or the future to measure the present. And to most supervisors this is unrealistic. Is it any wonder, then, that the supervisor so often perceives the activities of the controller as "perpetual needling," "shots in the arm," or "hammers waiting to hit you on the head"? Moreover, that he needs such stimulation and would be lost without it is an insult to his integrity. Instead of spurring him on, such activities often tend to anger him.

Because shop supervisors see these standards which controllers provide as unrealistic, rigid, and failing to take into account the concrete realities of their situations, their solution to the problem is also clear. Although stated more colorfully and less precisely than the controller's solution to these same problems, their direction is not too different. In the language of the shop, the solution lies in giving these "sarcastic bastards" who have a too-exalted opinion of their importance a "taste of factory life." They should be taught that their figures are not final, and how to see the other person's point of view. They also should be "untaught" a few things — for example, (1) that everyone besides themselves is lazy and wants to do as little work as possible; (2) that the best way to raise production is through pressure; and (3) that they are superior to factory people.

Granted that I have oversimplified the picture a great deal, I have done this purposely to make vivid the two quite different frames of reference from which the activities of the controller can be viewed. What from one frame of reference is helpful and challenging becomes from another frame of reference interference and enervating. Now the question I want to consider is: How can we think and talk about these differences of perception constructively?

To me the most futile of all questions to raise is: Which one of these perceptions is right or wrong? The quest for the answer to this question only leads in my experience to more and more misunderstanding. It leads to trying to get factory people to think like controllers or to get controllers to think like factory people. But this is a hopeless goal. Nothing that we know about the behavior of people in an organized human activity allows us to make the assumption that such a goal is either possible, desirable, or necessary for the achievement of purpose. Part of these differences of perception is written into the social organization of any factory. They are inevitable. They are just as brute and stubborn facts of life and living as any figures the controller can produce. To deny them is just as foolhardy as to deny the economic realities to which the controllers point.

For me, then, the solution does not lie in trying to deny or obliterate these differences. It lies in the way these differences are administered. They have to be administered so that they are not maximized to the point where they make for real trouble. When is this point reached? When factory supervisors really think that the activities of the controller are carried on deliberately and intentionally to discredit and humiliate them is one such point. When controllers really believe that factory supervisors are deliberately and intentionally trying to sabotage their efforts is another such point.

In both these instances the secondary complication of these differences becomes harmful to the efforts of the total organization. In such cases a new dimension is introduced which causes bitterness. This secondary complication, however, is not inevitable. It can be prevented by wise administration of those differences of outlook which must inevitably occur in any organization. Let us note that these harmful secondary effects occur because the reality of the differences in perception is being denied.

Perhaps I can make my meaning clear by looking at five possible solutions to this problem which have been tried, including two I have already considered:

1. An attempt to train supervisors to understand the need for and use of cost standards;
2. An attempt to train accounting people in the ways of the shop;
3. Group discussions with supervisors in which the latter are allowed to participate in the setting of the standard;

4. Group discussions with supervisors in which the latter are allowed to express freely their feelings, attitudes, and differences as the first step in gaining their emotional acceptance to the standard; and
5. An attempt to train controllers in human relations.

Let me state briefly some of the merits and demerits of these five approaches.

The first solution — training supervisors in the need for and use of standards — seems to me to miss the important point of the problem. It assumes that the primary difficulty is due to a failure in understanding logically the need and use of standards, when more often than not it is due to an unwillingness and incapacity to accept emotionally the standard. Under the latter conditions *telling* people how they should think and feel is the poorest way of obtaining their emotional acceptance.

The second solution — training accounting people in the ways of the factory — would be an expensive and lengthy job. Moreover, it assumes that experience *per se* without a pair of glasses through which to look at that experience will produce the desired results. Too often an accountant in the shop, because of his previous training, will be provided with ample ammunition to reinforce his own attitudes and preconceptions about shop people. As a result he often will not learn from this approach the lesson he is supposed to learn.

The third solution — allowing supervisors to participate in the setting of standards — is workable if done with sincerity, skill, and understanding. Before going into this approach, however, controllers should be sure that their definition of the situation as covered by the word "participation" agrees with that of the supervisors. "Participation" is a good idea and one which in general we are all for, but in my experience it is a concept difficult to implement in behavior. Too often rituals of participation are substituted for the genuine article; and, when this occurs, supervisors do not like it.

The fourth solution — bringing supervisors together in small face-to-face groups in which ample opportunity is given them to ventilate their old attitudes and feelings as a first step in the process of "unfreezing" them — is an approach which for me has a great deal of merit. It addresses itself directly to what I consider the central problem of getting people's acceptance to change. It is dealing directly with those variables which are controlling in the situation — the attitudes, feelings, and values of people. It recognizes and accepts differences of perception. The weakness in this approach is that it requires understanding, skill, and patience on the part of the person who leads such discussions. In my experience the results to be obtained can go no further than the understanding and skill of the discussion leader.

For this reason I should like to recommend a fifth approach to go hand-in-hand with the fourth. This would be to give training to controllers in human relations. Such training should be focused on getting the controllers to see, feel, and understand the consequences of their behavior for others. Until this problem is seen and felt in its full depth and complexity, controllers can never understand why their control systems can never work automatically and impersonally and why they will always have to be *administered* in terms of people and their relationships to each other.

In these last two suggestions I see the trend which the development of controllers might take. In such a development controllers would have to learn to see themselves more as *administrators* than as *technical specialists*. They would have to learn to become better listeners and to practice the art of appreciating and accepting points of view different from their own. They would have to learn to become better discussion leaders. In this way they would become gradually oriented to the administrative point of view. In my view, the technical specialist has to face up to and accept responsibility for only *some* of the consequences of his behavior, generally only the good ones. The administrator, on the other hand, has to face up to and accept responsibility for *all* the consequences of his behavior. This, as you know, is what makes his job tough, but also a real challenge.

Conclusion

I should like to consider several of the points mentioned by my coauthors.

At the heart of the problem of educational background lies a fundamental difference in concept which the educator has to face before he starts on his part of the job. To put it in the form of a question, is the controller to be regarded as a specialist, with skills different from the other executives in the business, or is he to be primarily regarded as a businessman whose assignment in the business is to make the figure function a real part of the management operation of the business?

This shows up in the debate which is currently going on among some of the professional organizations and into which the educators have been drawn. Specifically, there has been quite a lot of discussion going on as to whether special programs should not be prepared, separate curricula developed, and even separate schools established for the development of controllers. The proponents of such special training even look to a separate degree, perhaps an MCA, Master of Controller Administration; or to a certificate to be gained upon passing an examination, with certificate letters, such as CIA, Certified Industrial Accountant.

In most of the proposals so far, there has been the recognition that the proposed controller would be expected to know something besides accounting. He would be expected to know something about marketing, production, finance, human relations, and law. This would seem to imply that the controller is to be an administrator.

At the same time, quite a few people — without necessarily agreeing on the subjects which should be included for the education of a good controller — approach the question of the development of a controller with the idea that he is a *professional* man, somewhat analogous to a medical man or a lawyer. But if this includes special schools and degrees, it implies a specialized concept, which denies the idea that the controller is a professional man primarily in the art of administration and only secondarily in his technical position.

Now, I recognize that there is real value in professional status and in recognition of professional attainment. In this whole area, it seems to me that we should feel perfectly free to give recognition to the fact that a knowledge of the anatomy of control and a basic understanding of accounting are essential. I feel strongly about this; I think that sometimes, in our zeal to support the attitude that the controller is an administrator, we are inclined to feel that he should have no skills at all. There are two sides to this question, and it is not necessary to deny either.

But there is need to strike a balance. And I should like to urge all who are members of professional organizations that, when these proposals about special curricula and even special schools for training professional controllers come up for discussion and action, very serious consideration be given as to whether they really point in the direction in which a controller should be developed.

This leads to another facet of the problem, revolving around the highly different order of skills which the controller quite often is supposed to possess. He really has two quite different jobs in many, many companies. On the one hand, he is the personal consultant to the president or to other line executives, and as such he is somewhat of a staff financial advisor. On the other hand, he is a line executive with the responsibility for directing the work of perhaps thousands of employees in his department, with an investment in equipment running oftentimes into hundreds of thousands of dollars.

As the line head of this department, he has to have specialists under him. He must have a specialist in accounting forms and procedures, a specialist in tax problems, a specialist in consolidation work and SEC forms, perhaps even a specialist in electronic computing machines (their use requires a high degree of technical knowledge that takes some time to acquire).

The pressure of this functional arrangement, where the departmental head does have to administer specialized areas, on the one hand, and act as a personal president's consultant, on the other, seems to widen the gap between the top man in controllership and his assistants. I have been very much impressed by the number of companies, including many large companies, in which there really is no second man ready as a replacement. At the next level the people in the organization seem to be primarily specialists; and quite often, in many companies, when the controller dies or retires or moves to a different company, management has to bring in a controller from another company or hire their favorite CPA. All too often this is the pattern.

As my coauthors have indicated, there are many ways of developing controllers more purposefully. One is the idea of job rotation. In the controller's area particularly, this has some limitations attached to it. A tax expert may be a very good tax expert, but he may not be interested in any other department, may not even be interested in normal promotion; and the same thing may be true of other specialists. Again, if you try to rotate department heads, you may find that they may be able to handle other departments, but it may take too long a time and the cost may be too great.

Another approach is to have several second-level men in the controller's department, who operate on special assignments and whose job is to keep the controller posted and prepare reports for him to present to other executives. Of course, this too has a price tag, and runs the danger of developing "Crown Prince" complexes, which many companies like to avoid.

Also, where feasible, advantage can be taken of the very real benefits which exist in a decentralized operation. Each division controller shares the same kind of experience as does the top controller in the main office. He develops the ability of organizing his work and of fulfilling the control concept working with and for the other executives in the division. His experience more nearly parallels the experience of the top man than is possible in any other organizational setup. Through such a plan the top controller and his staff have an opportunity to watch the various division controllers as they carry on a rounded job and not as the heads of a specialized function.

But let me close this chapter on a different — or, perhaps I should say, further — note. It is one thing to develop controllers, difficult as it is. But once you get a good one developed that far, why should he not go still farther? Aren't the functions of the controller so important that it is desirable for a president to go through them before assuming the job of chief executive of the company? In a very real sense, controllership is the very fabric of business; it is the common denominator that is woven through all of business. If a controller can get on top of that, it is a natural thing for him to move into the presidential chair. And quite a few controllers have.

HOW TO DEVELOP FINANCIAL EXECUTIVES

Charles C. Abbott, Boyd N. Everett, William H. Lang, and Robert M. Hornung

It is a matter of common observation that during the last two or three years, perhaps longer, there has been a very large and growing interest in the business world in the subject of executive development, or executive training, or intracompany training programs, whatever the phrase should be.

This topic, of course, falls under the general heading of Adult Education, and as I have watched the success of the Advanced Management Program at the Harvard Business School and the great interest and considerable number of Harvard Business School faculty members who have done consulting work of one kind or another in this area — and there has been an astonishing number of them the last year or two — I have asked myself from time to time why this development should appear at this particular time.

Frankly, I have never been able to arrive at any very clear answer as to why there should be this great burst of interest in these different kinds of adult education and training just at this time. It does seem to me, however, that this new development is indirectly connected with two phenomena:

(1) As we all know, of course, the decade of the 1930's was, generally speaking, a decade of surpluses — a surplus of goods and

NOTE: Mr. Abbott is Converse Professor of Banking and Finance, Harvard Business School; Mr. Everett is Vice President and Treasurer, Continental Assurance Company; Mr. Lang is Assistant Treasurer, United States Steel Corporation; and Mr. Hornung is Vice President, National City Bank of Cleveland.

The introductory remarks are by Mr. Abbott; Mr. Everett discusses the development of financial executives in the insurance business; Mr. Lang discusses the problem from the point of view of a manufacturing or nonfinancial company; and Mr. Hornung considers the training of a banking executive.

commodities, a surplus of machines, and a surplus of people looking for work. In contrast, the decade of the late 1940's and early 1950's is clearly a period of shortages of many kinds, including competent and skillful personnel.

The transition from a decade of surpluses to a decade of shortages not only took place rather rapidly but was somewhat concealed by the war, when, of course, everyone expected a lot of shortages. And, since many of us were conditioned in the 1930's to a more or less chronic surplus of one kind or another, perhaps it never occurred to us, or perhaps we have just been a little slow in realizing, what the situation has been in recent years — namely, what seems to be, in certain areas at least, particularly management, a considerable shortage of personnel.

The human animal, of course, when confronted with a shortage of any type, always makes every effort to do the best he can with what he has — in the old New England phrase, to "make do." And it seems to me in one sense that this interest in adult education and executive development is simply a particular manifestation of this idea of trying to do the best you can with what you have.

(2) The other phenomenon to which this upsurge in executive development seems to be related is the astonishing growth of the economy in the postwar period. Basically, to me, this growth reflects, and is likely to continue to reflect in the future, the really extraordinary rate of population growth resulting from the upward change in the birth rate.

But, be that as it may, the more I have thought about this topic, the more different facets or aspects it seems to have, and the larger the number of topics that apparently might appropriately be related to it. It is impossible, here, to cover all sides of the question, but at least we can point up some of the more important aspects.

There is first, of course, the question of how to prepare men to be any kind of executives — not just financial executives, but sales executives, production executives, and so on. What types of substantive knowledge should they acquire, and what is the nature of that elusive thing called the "executive point of view"? This is a matter which has been discussed in detail in Part I of this book.

Then, obviously, there is the problem of how to bring men along in an organization after they have had some sort of preliminary or basic training. Here, it seems to me, a whole range of questions present themselves:

How can you foster and widen their experience?

How can you induce them or force them to take responsibility — safely, that is?

How do you keep them from being frustrated?

How do you keep them happy and contented, and bring them along?

All of these things in some measure enter into the problem of how to create and maintain an organization into which it is desirable for young men to go.

I was talking with one of my colleagues at the Harvard Business School not so long ago about this general problem of training executives, and, significantly, the question which came immediately to his mind was this one about the creation and maintenance of an organization into which it is desirable for a promising young man to go. It was very clear to him, he said, that the great bulk of companies could be divided into two categories: those into which one would advise young men to go, and those into which one would not advise promising executive candidates to go.

Another significant topic is the question of the relationship of the chief executive in an organization to the training of executives at lower echelons in his company. And on this point, of course, there are many theories about what the relationship should be, and how this operation should be conducted.

One of these theories is that the chief executive should do his best to develop the people under him as one of the measures to create an effective organization; that one of his principal jobs and responsibilities should be to see that the individuals under his supervision have every opportunity to recognize their fullest potentiality and, insofar as possible, be successful in their own right. I think the basic implication of that procedure is that if the chief executive makes successes of all the persons in his organization, he will almost automatically become a success himself.

Another of the many approaches to this problem is the general theory that any sound organization should have carefully developed planning schedules and replacement schedules, and that it is the responsibility of the chief executives to see that there are replacements all the way down the line.

That is an admirable idea. There is no question but that it is appropriate and desirable and proper in a large organization. But it is clearly inapplicable to a medium-size or small operation. In a great majority of the businesses in this country, it is probably impossible to have any highly developed schedules of replacements always on hand.

To return, however, to the specific subject of this chapter — the development of financial executives. Clearly we should look both at the training of executives in financial institutions and at the training of financial executives in nonfinancial institutions. Here one of the most provocative questions is whether the training is or should be identical in both types of organization.

I am well aware of the general proposition that a good executive is a good executive — whether he is in sales, or finance, or production; whether he is in a business corporation, a hospital, a university, the Army, or any other type of organization. But I am not entirely clear that the training which is desirable for a treasurer of a mercantile sales corporation is exactly the training desirable for an officer in a commercial bank.

In some commercial or primarily nonfinancial companies, for example, the financial work seems to be a thing apart from other kinds of operation, such as sales and production, and there is no very evident road into it, or no very clear road from it. It is a highly important and in fact an essential operation — as well as one requiring a high degree of skill — but I am not quite sure that it is as logically related to sales and production, say, as sales and production may be related to each other.

And even in financial institutions themselves, I sometimes have a feeling that types of work which may be extremely important — for instance, the management of the bond portfolio in a commercial bank — are not particularly closely related to other aspects of the operation of those financial institutions.

Thus, the fact that the financial work is perhaps set off a little from other parts of the operation, both in nonfinancial and in financial corporations, is one aspect of this problem of training financial executives.

Let us now examine this whole problem, first, from the point of view of the financial executive of an insurance company, then from the point of view of the financial executive in a nonfinancial company, and finally from the viewpoint of the banker.

Continental Assurance Company

Before we can discuss the training of an executive, we should know something about the nature of his job. The chief concern of the financial executive in the insurance business is with investments. Although he may have a few other functions, 90 per cent to 95 per cent of his time is spent on the investment end of the business.

In handling investments there are two separate and distinct functions: (a) the design and execution of policy, and (b) the selection and supervision of securities.

Design and execution of policy require a very thorough understanding of the mechanics and problems of the insurance business. One of the primary concerns is the effect of cyclical influences on particular types of insurance. For the problems involved in the life insurance business are very different from those of the casualty business or the fire insurance business.

To understand the design and execution of policy, the financial executive should have some working knowledge of the operating end of the business. For example, he cannot possibly work out a financial policy which will suit the casualty business unless he knows what can happen to that casualty business under different conditions or business cycles, or what hazards it is subject to, or the demands that may be made upon him as financial executive to provide either income, on the one hand, or liquidity, on the other hand.

The other function, securities selection and supervision, requires a combination of technical training, imagination, and judgment — a combination of qualities rarely found in one individual. But at least we do not want more than that! Knowledge of the insurance business itself is not a prerequisite for this part of the job.

But to reach the executive level the man at the top must be able to "get the show together." Because most security analysts come up strictly through analytical work in brokerage houses, investment banking houses, or banks, they rarely know very much about the insurance business. For example, I remember how, when I first went into the business 16 years ago, I knew almost nothing about it, and I had to start from scratch and practically educate myself in it.

Because top men in a company realize that they must have a man who understands insurance if he is going to design policy, and because they find no one among the security analysts who knows anything about insurance, they frequently pick their financial executives from other positions in the company — choosing men with no previous training in analyzing securities.

What can be done about correcting such a situation, that is, seeing to it that men are trained both in the insurance business and in security analysis before they reach the executive level? I believe that the situation can be corrected but that it cannot be done quickly. In fact, I have tried to correct it myself in my own company. I have not gone as far yet as I should go, but I suggest the following basic program for preparing a man in the securities analysis end of the business to take an executive position:

(1) The candidate should be encouraged to do as much off-the-job study as possible, either by reading, or by taking outside courses, or by taking courses provided within the organization. It would not be difficult for a company to set up a training course required for security analysts, which would meet for an hour once or twice a week. Each session or two, as necessary, could be conducted by the head of one of the departments in the company. He would describe from beginning to end the work of his particular department, telling about the insurance that his department writes, breaking down the costs of operation, outlining the hazards and the influence of the business cycle on those hazards, and describing the effect of volume on the operating statement.

In addition, of course, informal discussions might be conducted by department heads, and by the top executives themselves, which would bring the question of policy more to the front in the minds of these people. While the executives might not want to discuss all matters of policy design in this way, a great deal of it could and should be discussed.

(2) Another helpful practice is to have regular conferences, in which the financial executives discuss with all the members of the department the things that have been done over the past week, or the past month, or whatever period is decided upon, pointing out how those particular things that were done, say, security purchases, were fitted into the insurance business as opposed, perhaps, to some other kind of business. Most security analysts will find these programs invaluable, for they enable the analysts to gain a good knowledge of the insurance end of the business.

(3) There is another plan which might be considered, although in visiting other insurance companies, I do not yet find it widely used. It is the broad mingling of security analysis people, junior department heads, or whatever they are called, in nonoperating hours. A few years ago, in my company, we set up what we call the Continental Mid-Day Club. It is a luncheon club, and anyone can belong to it. We do have dues, which limits it a little in the sense that a number of the younger members usually do not choose to pay the dues, but as many join as possibly can. The juniors find that they can go to the club for lunch and sit around the tables with members of the other departments where they can talk about what is being done in this or that department. Sometimes the men play cards during the lunch hour, but for the most part there is talk of what goes on in the company. Moreover, they should be encouraged not to sit just with the people whom they have worked with all morning, but rather to sit with others in the company. Such an arrangement can be very useful in getting them to understand the business that is going on elsewhere.

Thus far the emphasis has been on developing executives within the company. But how do you select these men in the first place, at the beginning level? If we are going to train our security analysts to become financial executives responsible for the design of policy, we must start with good security analysts. How do we find them?

We in our company have a rather simple philosophy of selecting men. We feel that we cannot choose men on the basis of one or two or three interviews and be sure that we are getting the right man for our particular kind of work. So we hire an excess and weed them out. The work requires, as I have said, an unusual combination. I have always maintained that a good analyst has to be a combination of cynic and skeptic. He has to have imagination. He has to be inquisitive. He has to have a mathematical mind. And he has to have a basic accounting training. That last requirement is the only technical training we insist upon.

Of course, if a man applied to me for a job and appeared to have the requisite natural talents but lacked the necessary technical training in accounting, I would not rule him out altogether. If he assured me that he was willing to learn the technical aspects, either by going to night school or by studying accounting some other way, out of office hours, I should be in favor of hiring him on a trial basis. Here is where a background of general business education might help him, for it would tend to speed up his process of picking up the specialized accounting that he needs. But, even so, he would not be given very much responsibility or get very far in the department until he mastered accounting fundamentals, because he simply could not read a financial statement without it.

When a man comes in to start with us, we say:

> We don't know whether you are going to be able to do this work, but we will find out soon. I will make you only one promise, and that is that the very minute I or my associates decide that this is not the work for you, we will let you know, so that you can go on your way before it is too late to go somewhere else.

Now of course that is very easy to say, and it is very difficult to do. However, if you make yourself do it the minute you reach such a conclusion about a man, everybody is better off, and the company can afford to try more people.

But how do we decide, for example, whether or not a man can select securities successfully? We have no predetermined objective standard of satisfactory security selection, based on performance—like par in a golf game. The method which seems to work best is what I call the stimulation of ideas. In other words, to me a man shows that he is developing and coming along in the business if he keeps coming up with ideas, some of which are useful and, in the long run, profitable.

We have not been able to work out any scoring on it, because sometimes a person just happens to recommend an investment which would have been extremely profitable if we had bought more of it. And another time, as it turns out, the man's idea was probably less good, but we happened to buy a lot of it. It is a fairly difficult thing to measure. But when we get to know our men, we can tell over a period of time which ones are the ones that are coming up with ideas that work. And the ones who do not come up with any ideas are the ones we have to make up our minds to get rid of.

We have insisted that our analytical department always be larger than the needs of the business. We always plan so that we have some surplus. And in that way we can, you might say, have a selection process that works automatically, without our ever being shorthanded.

Of course, there is a certain risk in following such a policy. There is the danger that the existence of a larger than necessary group of analysts or junior financial executives may stifle individual initiative and interest because of limited opportunities for promotion. But this risk is more theoretical than actual.

Actually, in my company we have grown at a rate which has permitted us to give people responsibilities more rapidly than perhaps in other cases. When I first came with the company, all of our companies together had assets of only about $50 million. Now we have $500 million. And in the course of increasing our business, we have been able to find spots for a lot of people.

But there is danger in having too large a department if you do not have the courage to weed out people as fast as you make up your mind that they do not have the peculiar and particular requirements for this work.

As for the ones who are there on a permanent basis, who know they have been accepted and are moving forward, a department is not necessarily any larger than we need at any time. The one or two or three extra are those who perhaps are coming and going. That is what I mean by having a department larger than you need. Actually, it rarely happens that we get a department that is really larger than we need, but we did get into that situation about three years ago. It was after the war, and we had taken on a lot of people. We had some pretty good ones, and it got to the point where we were a little overstaffed. Quite frequently, about once a month or so, somebody from another company comes to me and wants to know whom he can get to do an analytical job on securities. So in this instance I recommended one of my men, and he got an excellent job out of it, better than the one he had with us. If we get to that point again, where I feel that my department is a little overloaded, I know I can find men other jobs outside the department. There really is no problem if you have men with ability.

There is one other point which I should like to touch upon. That is the question of incentives. The need for money incentive, of course, is something that you cannot dodge. If you want to find financial executives, you must pay them adequately. But that in itself is not sufficient. You must give them their incentive in the form of responsibility.

Too many of the companies I know hire a number of people and hand them out work to do much as they provide work for a typist. They do not give them any responsibility, and they do not give them a chance to do things for themselves.

Now, it is hard to do all these things at once, but you can do one particular thing, and that is to send the young men out on interviews. Send them out to companies in which your firm has investments, and give them a chance to talk with people in those companies. We find that this is very helpful for building morale.

Then a little later you may assign them to write up loan agreements. Surely you may find it desirable to revise these agreements, and you may say after the task is finished: "I could have done this thing myself in less time than I spent on those men." But the fact that the loan agreements then become their babies, so to speak, is very helpful to their morale.

There is an old saying about "letting them win some of the time." It makes them feel good, and I think it goes a long way toward the objective of giving them a feeling of responsibility.

If your young analysts are trained in policy design and are able to take responsibility, you will have a much stronger investment department, and you will minimize the conflicts that are likely to arise between your finance committee and your investment analysts. Furthermore, your investment department can take more responsibility in purchasing securities.

For example, over a long period of years, I have succeeded in obtaining a much greater degree of autonomy for the investment department in my company than I think exists in any other insurance company—at least any other with which I am familiar. Our investment department has the right to buy any security which can be sold.

In other words, we can buy before going to the finance committee. I happen to be a member of the finance committee. We meet once a week. In the interim periods between meetings we can buy any security which is marketable. Then, later, if the finance committee does not approve what we have bought, we must sell it.

This arrangement enables us to take advantage of opportunities as they present themselves in the securities market. Sometimes, decisions have to be made immediately, and price advantage may be lost by the time a committee can meet and act on the transaction.

I realize that this is not common practice in the insurance industry, but I think that when a finance committee can get sufficient confidence in its investment department to be able to do this, it will have much better results.

Once in a great while, no more than twice in the 16 years that I have been treasurer of the company, a committee has disagreed with the decisions of an investment man, and we have turned around and sold something.

I can remember one of those situations which occurred long enough ago so that the results can now be assessed. It turned out in that instance that the committee was wrong. But the committee is entitled to make a mistake once in a while, too, just as the individual investment people are entitled to make mistakes. In retrospect, I can think of others that I wish they had vetoed.

Not everything we buy is profitable. It is the over-all picture we have to consider. The investment man is bound to make mistakes once in a while and his superiors and associates should accept that fact. Also, he is bound to have ideas that are not accepted. He must be a big enough man to be able to say, "Well, I still think so, but that is the way it has got to be," and then go about his business.

I do not think it hurts a man's morale to disagree with him some of the time. The danger comes when you "knock him down" all or most of the time. If a man is beaten down by having 75 per cent of everything he suggests turned down, of course he is going to begin to feel frustrated. If it develops later that he was right most of the time about those suggestions that were turned down, his morale will definitely be hurt. We have run across that problem.

I believe in letting the men in the department win once in a while, even when I think they are wrong, without going to a committee. And some of the time — in fact, I guess probably at least half of the time — they are right and I am wrong. The important thing is to know your men and make sure you give them enough encouragement. And if you find that you are disagreeing with a man all the time, you might as well get rid of him, because neither you nor he can operate on that basis.

The good investment man will profit by his own mistakes. Occasionally an analyst will continually have "bright ideas," developed from thorough and seemingly sound analysis, which do not turn out successfully a majority of the time. When that occurs, you should go over the whole situation with him after the results are in and the soundness of his ideas has been determined. You should say to him, "Where in your analysis did you make the mistake? What was wrong with it? What changed after you made the analysis (if there was a change)? Or what didn't you see?"

If you can do that a few times, the incidence of these cases should decline. If they do not, then you have just made a bad choice, and your man is one of those fellows who has no judgment. He has ideas, but no judgment.

It is a difficult thing to find a man with the brilliant imagination and also the judgment to know the good ideas from the bad ones. But usually I find that if a fellow is intelligent and has imagination, we can train him to think a little more logically and to attain the necessary judgment in time. But the fact that he makes some mistakes should not be held against him. That is how he develops into a good financial insurance executive.

United States Steel Corporation

It is quite timely now that we should discuss the effectiveness of financial executives. For the last few years we have had a relatively easy time of it. Our collections have been good. Our credit risks have been minimized. It is only recently that money has become tight. Bankers are now beginning to do what many salesmen did over a period of years — hand out ration tickets.

With this change in the picture — with money scarce and expensive, and becoming more so — our financial people must be alert and ingenious in the procurement of money. They must also be more astute in the using of available money.

To be effective, the financial man should operate more efficiently in the face of this shorter supply of funds. He should improvise much as the purchasing department has had to do the last few years. This means two things, basically:

(1) He must make our present cash and cash resources do double duty. He must provide better supervision of credit policies, proper collection policies, elimination of lags in cash deposits, and shortening of the processing of cash.

(2) He must provide innovations in securing new cash, or retaining cash. The financial executive, to be effective, should continue to preach and implant in the minds of company management that there are rewards for operating on lesser investments in inventories, space, and so forth.

With this introduction to the job of the financial executive of an industrial company today, let us consider how we can select the right man for the task. The problem is threefold: (a) What are the qualifications of the job? (b) How do we spot the man with the necessary qualifications? (c) How can we make that man effective? To illustrate, let us assume that we wish to fill the position of assistant credit manager. But remember that it might just as well be the assistant controller or a placement in another phase of finance.

These are the qualifications that we think are important in these types of financial people:

1. Contact personality.
2. An analytical mind, a mind which understands and interprets figures, a mind that knows how to reason with figures in such a way that they are convincing; for figures can influence company management.
3. An educated mind, with a knowledge of accounting, business law, economics, and statistics.
4. Sound judgment, which I cannot define, but it is evident when you observe a person handling his work.
5. Ability and willingness to make decisions.
6. Acceptance of responsibility.
7. Ability to think and talk on his feet.
8. Ability to write clearly and forcibly.
9. Ability to secure respect and confidence.
10. Imagination and intellectual curiosity.
11. Desirable personal characteristics, integrity, appearance.

The next topic is how we try to spot this man. Either he is already on the job or he is a new young man just starting to work for us. What things do we look for?

1. Aptitude for work and accomplishment; determination to take on any assigned job and complete it.
2. Ability to function at maximum speed on a minimum of rest and recreation; and, by the same token, ability to relax in these hectic days.
3. Appreciation and understanding of the point of view, the interests, and the needs of other people, without becoming emotionally involved and without losing the objectivity which one must maintain.
4. The quality which assures one's acceptance as a leader by subordinates, a person to whom the subordinates will look for decision and for leadership.
5. Ability to direct one's energies and attention constructively and industriously to his work.
6. Acknowledgment of personal limitations, and readiness to accept constructive suggestions from one's superiors in order to improve his own performance.
7. Emotional stability.

Once we have found the person with the necessary qualifications, our next step is to make him effective. For it is not enough to have the qualifications. They are merely the raw material — the basis for becoming effective. They must be developed and used if executive effectiveness is to be obtained. I am going to assume, first, that our organizational structure is a sound one; and, secondly, that we have good basic manpower to work with. The problem will vary depending on whether the individual is new in the organization or is a veteran employee with a new assignment who is being revitalized or being challenged by his new job.

In either case, our first approach is what we call "clearing the air" — making the man comfortable, to make sure that he understands and appreciates the new situation in which he finds himself. This involves such simple things as having him appreciate the company objectives and the objectives of the particular department where he works.

He should know the areas of responsibility of his department, to the end that he can tie in his personal relationships with the company-at-large, as well as with others in his own department. He must determine an area for his own contribution to the department.

We want to eliminate from his mind in a manner satisfactory to him those things which are beyond his control. This is not to deny him an interest in extraneous matters, but to provide him with a basis for evaluating and emphasizing the fundamental of "first things first."

We must go on to find out his capacity. What do we expect of our executives? We expect them to be able to think clearly, to be willing to make decisions, and to assume responsibility. The employee tangibly and definitely is tied into his departmental organization. The importance of the employee's assignment creates an atmosphere which emphasizes the importance of the individual. It gives him an interest in his job, which is a primary requirement. This, we believe, is the healthy attitude for growth of the individual's thinking, for the accuracy of his work, and for the acceptance of the responsibility which is placed upon him.

Next, assuming the employee's capacity for growth has been established and his interest has been aroused, it becomes necessary to explain what the job is in specific and individual terms. Effort is made to personalize the work assigned him — not only to demonstrate how it is to be done, but also to show that there is delegation of responsibility and authority.

Then, we must create opportunities for practice. We are desirous of seeing the individual in action. We want to determine how the individual is handling or is going to handle his assignment. We must give the individual the opportunity for decision making, and for creating the pleasure which is inherent in the use of authority for one's own operation. In other words, the man must have the desire to make his own decisions and recognize the need for making them. And he must recognize also that there are penalties as well as pleasures that go with the acceptance of responsibility and authority.

Someone has described the delegating of authority as that operation which permits the opportunity for mistakes. In other words, the supervisor should not breathe down the man's neck in checking on details. He should judge him on the basis of the quality of the finished product.

Finally, the employee is ready to be introduced to a concept that is fundamental in our organization. I imagine many have other names for it, but we call it "management by exception." Very briefly, this is the practice of letting a man work out his own method of operation within the guideposts that have been laid down. It has mutual advantages.

For the employee, it means that as long as he is operating within broad, established policies which he understands, and is personally satisfied with his own work performance, he is the boss and is running his own show.

For his supervisor, it means that there is a basis for observing the employee's judgment and ability, determined by the nature of the problems which the employee refers to him as exceptions to the assigned task or to general policies.

This is a keystone upon which effectiveness in our organization is being sought — assuming, of course, that a man of the necessary capacity has been placed on the job. To us, it means primarily a follow-up and a review of the work accomplished to determine, first, the ability of the individual for the work assigned, and, secondly, his attitude toward the organization, toward his co-workers, and toward his job. It is the supervisor's job to set up the guideposts for the subordinates, and they, in turn, have to spend enough time to see that the employees know what standards of performance are requisite.

The important thing is to define a man's responsibility and say, "Here is your job," and then let him operate within that field. In our experience this is the best way to develop effectiveness.

Let me conclude on a more general note. Today, more than ever, we need executive effectiveness. It is not enough to rely on years of experience and factual knowledge to develop our men into responsible executives. We must have a well-designed, a well-planned program if we are to overcome the shortage of executive personnel which faces us and meet the challenge of new conditions in the industrial world.

National City Bank of Cleveland

In the discussion of the financial executive of the insurance business, attention was centered on the people who handled investments — for that is the primary task of such financial executives. In the discussion of the financial executive in a nonfinancial company, we used as our example the assistant credit manager, to simplify our task and to make it more realistic. Here, in our consideration of the banker, I am going to follow the same procedure and for similar reasons. I am going to limit my discussion to the commercial loan officer — partly for the purpose of simplification and partly in recognition of the fact that his functions are the main stream of commercial banking.

A commercial loan officer serves as the focal point for the customers who deal with the bank. That is, the services to and from the customer flow through him. These include negotiation and administration of loans, the selling of a bank's services, and constant contact with the customer and his problems and his personnel, so the bank can have to a certain extent a continuing appraisal of the customer, whether an individual or a company. In the case of a company, the bank must be cognizant of its effectiveness as a competitive business.

Training the executive for the position of a commercial loan officer starts, of course, with recruitment and selection. Banking has probably not done a very good job of that in the last few years, or for a number of years.

For one thing, our selection of men has been handicapped by the fact that banking is not rated very high among young people getting out of school. When I graduated from the Harvard Business School 25 years ago, investment banking and commercial banking were high on the list of desirable professions, and a fair percentage of my class entered banking. That has now swung pretty much the other way, with the result that banks have sought people out of a relatively small number who were interested in banking.

Perhaps one of the reasons why banking has become less popular in recent years is the feeling that the training period in a financial institution consumes a longer time than in many merchandising or industrial concerns. I think this is a misconception. Recently, a New York bank published a survey which shows that more graduates who went into banking in 1947 reached the $7,500-and-over bracket by 1952 than the men who entered other businesses. Because the ranks are thin in banking, a number of men have attained executive standing in their twenties; many more of them become senior officers in their thirties.

There has also been a feeling that the salary level in banks is not competitive. I think this situation is being corrected rapidly. It has to be if we are to attract good people. Fortunately, the future is much brighter. With the freeing of interest rates in this country from a controlled market to a free market, it seems assured that banking will have better earnings, and there must be a correlation between the earnings of an industry and its ability to attract good people.

Another complaint is that young men in banking, even at the

junior executive level, are not given the responsibility and authority which are enjoyed by men in other industries at comparable salary levels. I think in years past this situation was true.

The many checks and balances which are set up in banks to protect their assets and the deposits of their customers have made it necessary to use great care in delegating responsibility to individuals. But, today, perhaps in response to the general recognition of the importance of giving responsibility to people if they are to develop into effective executives, there is a definite trend, particularly in large metropolitan banks, to make men responsible for their customer contacts and for the loans they make. Sometimes two or three officers are given a territory together and have full responsibility for loans made there; in fact they can commit the bank up to very large amounts of money.

Therefore, any feeling that the opportunities in banking for achieving positions of responsibility at competitive salary levels are few is definitely unfounded. There are plenty of opportunities for the qualified young man.

Now just what are the qualifications we look for in a man who is to become a commercial loan officer? Like everybody else, we try to get men with a good scholastic record. Also, we want some indication that the man possesses leadership ability. Poise, tact, pleasing personality, and a good appearance are things that go to make a good bank representative.

We also want a man who can get along well with the people with whom he is working. Too often we find that our young trainees feel that they are people apart — destined for big jobs. They spend all their time trying to impress the people several levels above and tend to look down on those just above them and also on the immediate job to be done. We want men who recognize the importance of each job as it comes along.

Once we have found our man we must train him. Let me go over briefly the methods generally used in banks to get a new person situated on the job.

The larger banks, of course, can have formal training programs. In some banks the people who are selected to go on the training program start in immediately upon hiring, but in others they are first put on a job in some productive service for a period of a year or two. In the formal training program the trainees usually go around to the various departments largely as observers. The purpose is to give them quickly a basic knowledge of banking and its various functions. The recruits may stay in a department from one day to a number of weeks. Frequently the trainee is required to prepare a written report on each department to make sure that he has learned what he is supposed to learn. He is taught by observing.

In smaller banks the training is done on the job; the man is rotated through a number of operating departments, and he is taught by actually doing the work of the department.

After going through the operating divisions, the trainee usually ends up in either the credit department or the investment department. In some banks those are now combined into one department. There he begins to get familiar with the bank's customers and some of their problems, to learn the processes of analysis, and to form some basis of credit judgment.

As one of its important steps, the work involves investigation. Initially it is of the indirect kind, consisting of exchange of information among banks, inquiries to suppliers, customers, and occasionally even competitors.

Then later on the direct investigation work begins. At first this work is with the smaller customers. The man is sent out to discuss a loan, to explore the needs of the borrower, to go over the entire business with the management, and to come back with an appraisal and recommendation. That is a very interesting job, and it usually starts with a case where the trainee is dealing with the top man in the business, the one who makes decisions, who knows the whole operation, and who usually can provide all the necessary information.

The period of time that the trainee spends in this work may vary from a relatively few months to some years, depending on the man, the bank, and the opportunities up the line. Some banks rush a man through in nine months or under, if he has been carefully selected; others take anywhere from one to five years. But eventually he is moved into a loan department. He may be assigned to a loan officer, or he may be brought in as a member of a loan group. In some banks these groups are set up on a territorial basis; in others, on an industry basis; and in still others, on a combination of the two. When the trainee joins the loan department, he is in the lower range of the executive group.

In the remainder of this chapter section I should like to describe some of the things that are being done and some others that perhaps could be done in order to increase the effectiveness not only of these recruits but of the people all the way up the line. I am thinking of executive training as a continuing process.

One of the important methods of improving executive effectiveness is to hold, periodically, meetings of officers and key people in the bank at which the chief executives discuss bank problems and policies. In our bank this is done whenever there is need for such discussion. It is part of the current idea of keeping the organization well-informed and working toward special goals.

We have a continuous program for studying credit problems. This program consists of talks and discussions led either by people inside the bank or occasionally by an outsider who comes in to discuss such subjects as business conditions, the business outlook, real estate markets, and consumer credit. Special emphasis is placed on the study of the money market, for a bank officer must be prepared to discuss it with his customers, and that is one of his more important services.

Probably more should be done in the way of human relations within the bank, particularly the many intricate problems of customer relations. That is something which I do not think has been handled very well by most banks. There are many different human relations situations that a banker runs into in the course of his work. I am sure that if the senior officers of a bank took some of their time and experience and wisdom to tell the younger men what kinds of problems the senior officers have run up against, and the various methods of meeting those situations, it would be most helpful.

Each man, of course, will handle the human relations problems he encounters in the light of his own experience and his own personality; but as he becomes familiar with the experiences of others and sees alternate methods, he will broaden out and be able to handle some very difficult situations better than he otherwise would.

A bank officer has to be a salesman. The chances are that when he entered banking, he was not a salesman and had to become one by training and by experience. If he had had a great urge to sell, I am quite sure he would not have gone into banking; or if he did get into banking, he probably would not have stayed there. So, those who stay in banking have to be indoctrinated with sales-mindedness. I think that banks all over the country are recognizing this problem and taking steps to solve it.

One method that has been quite useful is to review the successful cases of business acquisition to find out how the "sale" was made. This may mean examining all the steps that were taken over a period of years and trying to evaluate the ones that were successful, so that future sales effort can be directed along more intelligent lines.

In our bank we have tried a rather novel experiment in this area. We have called in the financial officers of friendly customers and asked them to give us their side of bank relations and solicitation. These men are exposed to solicitation from a great number of banks, and by having them tell us their reactions to the various sales efforts we get that rare opportunity of seeing ourselves as others see us. We learn what the other man wants to get from the bank officer, what he appreciates, what he endures, and what he would rather talk about. It might be an understatement to say that certain aspects of good customer relations are involved in these visits and invitations.

A bank officer has an opportunity to interview a number of different companies. He can learn a great deal about a great many businesses. In fact, the training he receives in the bank is very valuable if he should decide later to enter another type of business.

Furthermore, he has an opportunity to observe the varying ways in which companies handle their personnel problems, and can learn many lessons from what he sees. Some companies have very fine morale and teamwork. Let us take as an example an executive who goes into a company as a new man and inherits a team. If he takes the attitude, as many have done, that this is the team and he is going to make it do — which means that he will place confidence in it — he will build up its morale. If there is a replacement to be made, it usually comes from within; but if somebody does come from outside, he is probably accepted better than he would otherwise be.

On the other hand, we have seen managers who have very little confidence in their organization, who are always looking over to greener fields in other companies, wishing they had that type of men, and perhaps trying to take them into the organization. They do not expect much from their own organization, and, that being the case, they very seldom have an agreeable surprise from it.

As mentioned earlier, a bank has to carry on a rather continuous appraisal of its customers and their credit. I think the same thing should be done with its employees.

We would not think of lending a company money on an appraisal made some years ago. On the same basis we should not tag employees early in the game and let the tag stick; we should reexamine them periodically. People develop at different rates and in different ways, and some people, with a little aging, become more useful. That is certainly true of a bank's personnel.

Also, we should be on the watch for potential executive material among the lower levels in the bank — the tellers and bookkeepers, for example. By no means do banks always draw their executives from the college group. The American Institution of Banking is helping to supply the educational background for people with ability who lack the necessary prior schooling. Much of the work is offered in night courses. And many banks send their people to the Graduate School at Rutgers University or the Advanced Management Program at the Harvard Business School. This practice of helping to educate the men in the bank and thus bring along executives from within should be encouraged among banks — particularly in this period of shortage in financial personnel.

An awareness of other aspects of personnel relations is finding its way into banks today. Bankers are beginning to talk of trying to write job qualifications and job specifications for the senior ranks just as they have been doing for the clerical workers up through the branch-officer and junior-executive level. So far as I know, this has not been done very much until recently. In other words, banks are becoming aware of the importance of management evaluation and management inventory control.

In recognition of the potentials of these aspects of personnel administration, some banks have put senior officers in charge of enlarged personnel programs. It is recognized that this is definitely a problem for top management and that the responsibility for training should begin in the upper ranks of the bank.

There are many opportunities in which senior officers, especially, can give that little bit of extra training, take the extra moment to tell why, to explain, to encourage, to bring people along. A great deal more can be done along these lines. Banks often have been pretty cold places, and this attitude of trying to pull the other fellow along I am sure is a very rewarding one and helps to humanize banks.

Banking has a very important job to do in our economy, and it needs and will continue to need the best executive talent that it can recruit, train, and develop under a continuing program.

HOW TO INCREASE YOUR OWN ADMINISTRATIVE EFFECTIVENESS

Edmund P. Learned, John H. Martin, Robert S. McNamara, O. A. Ohmann, and Kenneth R. Andrews

What can each of us, as an individual, do on his own initiative to increase his competence as an executive?

That is the question which we shall focus on in this chapter, with the hope that every reader will be able to find some idea that he might be able to use himself — regardless of the position, the type of organization, or the particular industry that he represents. In other words, perhaps this discussion will provide an experience in self-orientation, although that will have to be determined by the way the ideas are applied.

The kinds of questions implied in our discussion — for we are not addressing ourselves directly to them — include:

What can an individual do to increase his competence as an executive?

How can he organize his work to increase his effectiveness?

How can an executive learn to see himself as others see him and measure his effectiveness from their point of view?

How can he increase his effectiveness through the development of subordinates?

How can an executive determine when and how to take action?

How can an executive develop a company-wide viewpoint regarding special problems assigned to him?

NOTE: Mr. Learned is Professor of Business Administration, Harvard Business School; Mr. Martin is President, United Lumber Yards; Mr. McNamara is Assistant General Manager, Ford Division (at the time of writing, Comptroller, Finance Department), Ford Motor Company; Mr. Ohmann is Assistant to the President, Management Development, Standard Oil Company of Ohio; and Mr. Andrews is Associate Professor of Business Administration, Harvard Business School.

Mr. Learned provides the introduction; Mr. Martin discusses the problem in the small company and Mr. McNamara in the large company; Mr. Ohmann develops the significance of attitudes; and Mr. Andrews and Mr. Learned provide the conclusion.

In the Small Company

I consider myself a representative of truly small business. I have about 150 employees in a group of retail lumber yards in small towns in California. There must be a great many more people who are and will be administrators in businesses of this size than there are in businesses with 10,000 employees, which I have heard some people call small.

I shall present my points as a case study drawn from my own experience.

The fundamental tenet of small business administration was well summarized by a friend of mine, also in the retail business, when I asked him how he got things done in his business. He replied: "It's easy. I can do anything in the store better than any of my employees."

That is not a particularly modest statement, but I honestly believe it can be generalized to other small businesses in the sense that the head man in a small business is likely to be the most effective operator *in the major activity* of that business — that is, the best salesman, in a retail business; the best machinist and engineer, in a small machine shop; and so forth. This is what I call the "best man" approach.

This in turn means that in a really small business the head man must completely and constantly administer a lot of overlapping functions.

I am afraid this position makes it a little difficult for the average business school graduate to become a small business administrator, particularly when he is first out of school. It is very easy while one is a student to become indoctrinated with the proposition that an administrator can always hire specialists for particular functions. Even if he can, without the "best man" qualification he will find it difficult to command the respect necessary to get the best results from employees.

My personal experience in this problem was particularly difficult because I came to a small business from the largest corporation in the world, the United States Government.

My initial problem was to find a substitute or modification of the "best man" approach. The obvious policy was to avoid injecting myself where I could not make a contribution — although even that, I discovered, was easier said than done.

The company was losing money, however, so it was clear I had to do something. At this point I became aware of what I think is a second safe generalization about small businesses: that there is a dearth of facts and figures available.

Executives in large corporations sometimes talk about the flow of data they analyze as a basis for making decisions. In our company a decision is an application of the "best man" approach. And, as is true in the average small concern, it is sometimes made by feel. I hasten to add that feel is often extremely good and produces excellent profits. But if the head man does not have that feel, or if his hunch gets on the wrong wave length, he has to have facts and figures.

Now, although a person presenting a case study should be careful about making unqualified remarks, I want to state categorically that there is no business so small that it cannot and should not have available the pertinent figures of its principal areas of activity even if the head man has to run his own adding machine. I would define the major areas of activity as being where the money is tied up and where the money flows in and out of the company in largest amounts. There is not much use worrying about a salesman's traveling expense of $1,000 a year if the $100,000 payroll has not been examined — yet so often it is done the other way around.

Another difficulty which I am sure all administrators face, whether they are in large or in small companies, is the problem of doing the job which needs to be done rather than the job which the principal administrator likes to do. For example, in our industry, by tradition — perhaps because it is a pleasant job — the head man generally does the buying. I do not want to disparage the importance of a good buyer, but I believe that in most cases the chief executive could be doing something else, even though it might be less attractive than the job of handing a salesman an order for something he is eager to sell.

Incidentally, this matter of selecting the jobs to be done brings me to a point which differs from the classic belief that an executive must free himself from the press of matters brought to him. While my experience may not be typical, it seems to me that even the lowest level administrator is likely to have more difficulty in defining the problems to be worked on than in freeing himself from the problems brought to him. Very few employees, if they have anything on the ball at all, carry their problems uphill — except the difficult tasks like deciding which person to let go in a cutback.

But let us return to the case study, which we left at a point where I was a new man in the company. In our company the major areas of investment are accounts receivable and inventory. It was easy to handle accounts receivable; everyone knew the consolidated figure should be kept as low as possible. The inventory, however, presented a considerably more complicated problem because of a conflict in merchandising philosophies. This conflict arose from a policy of trying to have on hand everything a customer might want to order versus a policy of getting a good turnover on every item.

Because I was not yet sufficiently familiar with the lumber business, I had to find a substitute for the "best man" approach, as I mentioned earlier. I found that by making extremely detailed figures myself from some of the general basic inventory data, I could go to even an experienced old-time yard manager and give him factual information on some of the specific items in his inventory which was helpful to him in reducing his inventory and turning it over. This contact served as a basis for coöperation on the part of the various yard managers in the over-all job of reducing inventory and consequently was far more effective than any amount of exhorting or ordering would have been.

At the same time, I learned what I thought was another worthwhile lesson — learned it as the result of a complete failure on my part — and that is not ever to present a new set of figures or a new approach to old figures without a full, even tediously detailed, explanation. For example, I devised a new ratio for keeping track of inventory and gross margin. It was a beauty. I tried it out and was convinced the results were reliable. However, when I showed it to my associates, almost the only reaction was, "Hasn't that man anything better to do than to play with his slide rule?" I had not prepared them for a new way of doing things by giving them a step-by-step explanation of how it worked.

This leads me to a comment on the matter of working with people, which is the heart of all administrative activity. In my opinion the principal limitation of a small business, in contrast to a large one, is that practically everyone in the company above the level of laborer has to be interchangeable. To put it another way, each one has to be a completely rounded person. But a human being just is not made that way; rather, he is a combination of strengths and weaknesses.

The larger companies, at least theoretically, put the individual in a more specialized task, thereby taking advantage of his strengths and minimizing his weaknesses. That is, they take the man who has an aptitude for sales and put him in sales, not on truck maintenance or bookkeeping.

In contrast, our small yard managers sell material, order in stock, keep books, collect on accounts, look out for their equipment, hire help, and in general conduct almost a completely rounded business. Our case may be a little extreme, but I believe the majority of small businesses have to accept a compromise of abilities in order to get the work done. It might be argued that this makes for better rounded businessmen in the long run. But, as we used to say in the big depression, you cannot eat the long run. We have to make profits today as well as ten years from today, and that takes a rounded executive right away.

I have also found it important to avoid giving people a label. For example, a few years ago we bought a small company and inherited a bookkeeper about 30 years old whom we kept on the job while the transition was being made. Afterward there was no place for him; he did not want to move to our accounting department which is in another city. About that time a manager of a small yard quit and we had a job to fill. Somebody made the very dubious suggestion that we put on the job this bookkeeper who had had no previous experience of this kind. The happy ending here is that a very average bookkeeper has turned out to be one of our best yard managers.

The point I am trying to make is that, with the exception of the extreme specialist, there is a great deal more versatility in people below the executive level than most of us are willing to recognize.

Now, let me make a controversial point. It may be heresy, but in my opinion the sacred tradition of lines of authority is pretty vague in a small business; and I do not think it is necessary for the small business administrator to adhere rigidly to such lines. In our company everybody at the working level generally expects the head man to give him answers, even though there are intermediary levels of authority. Furthermore, those on intermediary levels of authority expect him to give answers; and if he does not have the answers, they want to know why.

This leads to another tenet, one that I consider the No. 1 requirement of holding people's confidence in an organization: keep everyone in the organization informed. Even though news is bad, I prefer to tell it to my employees before they hear it secondhand.

Our physical setup, scattered as it is over a wide area, presents problems of frequency and type of contact with members of the organization. I believe thoroughly in Secretary Humphrey's famous phrase, to the effect that the best fertilizer is the footprints of the boss. At the same time, while it may be trite to say it, I feel strongly that the supervisor or administrator ought to take something worthwhile, wherever possible, to the person being contacted—ideas, suggestions, or merely a positive and sincere compliment on a particular job well done. Just dropping in to say "Hello" can easily lead to resentment if the person visited gets the idea his superior has nothing better to do than waste his time. Furthermore, a positive worth-while contact initiated by the supervisor is much more likely to generate pertinent questions or helpful suggestions from the employee than is small talk or constant criticism.

If a criticism has to be given, it should flow into the positive and specific of *what* the man failed to do and *why* it should be done another way. It cannot just be, "You're wrong," and "You should do it such-and-such a way." At the same time, any compliment honestly and sincerely given which is based on fact and performance cannot be overdone.

A good rule to follow is to explain to every employee with whom you work the objectives of his job and what he is expected to do, in a simple, direct statement. If you cannot state it in a simple way, something is wrong with your job description, and the employee's failure to carry it out is not completely his fault.

We have tried working out a manual for all of our major procedures and practices, but frankly it has not been particularly significant, except in some very detailed areas, like accounting, which depend on actual rules. In general, we have found it better to describe the job orally with specific detail.

Finally, what about the important question of getting action in a small company? We are all aware that the principal means of getting action is through people. This is a matter of incentives, of presenting opportunities for self-expression, learning to listen before telling, giving instructions that a man can understand, and so on — all of which are examples of good human relations. Since this subject is covered in some detail in the next section, I am going to touch only on one or two points where there may be some difference between the large and the smaller company in the matter of getting action.

One of these differences is what I like to call a one-at-a-time procedure. When the small business administrator picks out a job to be done, it is essential that it be pushed to conclusion as rapidly as is consistent with the type of problem faced. Most small business administrators simply cannot farm a job out to somebody and wait for reports on the results. The matter in hand has to be settled in the most effective way possible so that the next thing in line can be attended to.

In my experience, this often means an undue concentration on particular jobs for at least short periods of time. For example, a year or so ago, our accounts receivable got out of hand. I spent most of two months working with the yard managers on our accounts while I was looking for a new credit man. The result was that, by the time I found the new credit man, I had learned the accounts in some detail, and so now it is easy for me to appreciate whether he is doing his job. He turned out to be a good man, and I moved on to a new area.

I point out this example to emphasize that an administrator, to utilize the one-at-a-time approach, has to get each job out of the way or he will never get it done. One way to take care of this need for completing the job is by the oldest and one of the most effective devices ever invented — the simple piece of paper with jobs listed on it, kept on your desk, so that they face you every day. I tried scheduling jobs by dates but found it difficult to live with the schedule; the temptation was to give up jobs if their dates were not kept. You have to use your will power not to scratch them off as something you have decided you don't need to do after all. Now a job is not stricken from the list until positive action is taken and it is done. Each of my assistants has a similar list of jobs which have been assigned to him by mutual agreement.

Another device I tried was having regular weekly conferences, but I found that it was completely inconsistent with our basically informal approach. Now I simply ask my assistants about their progress on their job lists at irregular intervals; they know I am going to be asking, and the system works. In fact, quite a tribute was given me a month or so ago. One of my more outspoken assistants, in talking about this listing of jobs, told a new man, "It sometimes gets embarrassing when Mr. Martin asks about the same thing three or four times," but the part that pleased me most was that he smiled when he said it.

I have had one successful experiment in combining the big business conference technique with small business administration. I found that I was getting nowhere in leading our men in our principal activity, which is selling. The reasons were obvious. I not only did not know our products, but I lacked experience as a sales manager in the "best man" conception. Consequently what good ideas I might have picked up from a competitor or read in a magazine did not make any impression on my men.

So, in order to pass on these ideas effectively and stimulate others to action, I decided to set up a conference system whereby we would have a regular monthly meeting of our four yard supervisors and two yard managers for a full discussion of all sales and merchandising ideas. Each specific idea agreed upon is listed together with the name of the man responsible for carrying it out. This explicit assignment of responsibility is very important. At the next meeting the man reports what action has taken place.

We ran into difficulty at the beginning — a problem I want to emphasize — because the working sales people seemed to think that these meetings were on a lofty plane and that they should result in grand and profound truths! It took a series of meetings to put over the fact that what we wanted was specific, detailed suggestions that could be carried out the next morning. But the idea finally sank in. And now we have a conference system developed that has become very successful — a system whereby the men who decide that a certain idea is workable are also the men who translate it into action.

This may sound immature to readers who are in more formally organized businesses, but I think those in very small businesses will recognize that making any kind of formal technique work is rather a triumph.

I have tried to give a picture of a small business administrator at work. I have no grand conclusions to draw, but perhaps I can summarize:

(1) Unless the small business administrator possesses a great skill in the particular business, the problem of a substitute for the "best man" leadership is a major one.

(2) The administrator must take the initiative in selecting problems to be attacked, and the selection must be on need, not preference. The greatest concentration of investment and/or money flow is the best test.

(3) He should try to take something to subordinates on each contact.

(4) A great difficulty is the need to train general purpose men, not specialists.

(5) Specific jobs should be pushed to quick conclusions, since not much happens if the administrator sits back and waits for reports. Simple techniques such as listing jobs may be very helpful.

(6) Making a self-analysis — such as this one I have made for presentation here — can do a lot of good. I advise others to try the same thing.

In a Large Company

Let me point out initially that I do not believe there is any real difference between increasing one's administrative effectiveness in a small company and in a large company. I should like to pick up the note on which the preceding section ended — the need for self-appraisal, or at least the need to think about one's administrative effectiveness and then do something about it. In this connection, I want to make four general comments.

The first has to do with work selection. It has been my experience — and I am sure the experience of virtually every administrator — that the average executive faces far more work than he can possibly accomplish. His task, therefore, is to select from the work before him those particular jobs he will devote his attention to, and in general to develop a set of priorities with respect to those jobs. Before he can do this properly, he must decide what basis he will use in selecting the particular projects he plans to take care of.

It is very, very easy for an administrator to let his attention be trapped by the many pieces of paper that float across his desk or by the people who call him on the telephone or walk into his office. Far too frequently, by the end of the day little has been accomplished, and quite clearly the work of that day has been dictated by others rather than by the administrator himself.

I do not wish to imply that a day spent in talking with and listening to people is necessarily a day lost. That, of course, depends on what is being discussed — and also on what the executive's habits are. Many administrators (myself included) spend too much time this way simply because they are not as effective as they should be. If an executive has a clear formulation of his objectives in mind before he starts talking with his subordinates, I believe he will have taken the greatest single step to save his own time and also to avoid possible misunderstanding on their part.

In the preceding section attention was called to the fallacy of an administrator's allowing himself to do what primarily interests him or what best matches his particular abilities. Frequently an executive will find that his interest and abilities are not broad enough to encompass the total responsibility of the job, and the work load he chooses is dictated by personal interest rather than by the full requirements of the job. What usually happens in such a case is that the administrator falls into the trap of allowing a large part of the work of the organization to go by default.

There are plenty of stories of executives who operate on this theory — for instance, the vice president who spends perhaps an hour and a half every day shuffling through papers on his desk, stuffing them in envelopes, putting on stamps, and doing the easy jobs rather than the ones that demand attention, the tough jobs.

The question is, "What are the jobs that we have to do?" One useful rule that an administrator can and should follow is to select his work in relation to its effect on profit. When I say profit, I am thinking of it as a measure of management productivity. I am thinking of profit from the long-range point of view as well as in terms of its short-run contribution to the financial strength of the company. In our company, we try to follow the rule of rating a job by its effect on profit, and in discussions with our supervisors about selecting jobs to be done we have tried to emphasize the significance of this measure.

As an illustration of administrators' allowing themselves to pay attention to the less important rather than the more important — an example of our failure to use the rule of effect on profit as a basis for determining priority of work — let me point up a situation that holds in many companies. There is no problem that gets so much attention as the purchase, sale, or lease of a piece of property, regardless of size and nature and importance. A lease to pay as little as $1,000 a year cannot be signed without action from the board of directors, and the chances are that all the executives stopped work to spend a half-hour or so discussing the matter when it first came up. Yet a major purchase contract can slide through with practically no review; a change in production specifications or an advertising or sales promotion campaign requires little or no discussion by a major group of executives.

The next point I should like to make concerns the question of simplifying the administrator's job. I am perhaps presenting the viewpoint of a controller primarily, but I think 80 to 90 per cent of the decisions that have to be made on a day-to-day operating basis are decisions that require facts.

We have found it very effective to maintain simple, routine ways of obtaining and having on hand at all times the facts that serve us best for the 80 to 90 per cent of day-to-day operating decisions which can be based on such information. As an illustration, I carry in my pocket a set of cards that includes all of the operating information I need in order to make the day-to-day decisions coming to my attention.

One card, for example, covers all the economic factors that determine and limit our market, past and future. Another covers market trends and dealer stock information. Another carries all the specifications of our product versus that of our competitors. Another carries all the production schedules past and future. Another carries all cost and financial information and the financial results of our several divisions. Another carries all the prices of our products versus our competitors' prices. And so on.

These cards are relatively simple to maintain, and I use them frequently; rarely is there a decision that cannot be based on one or more of the facts readily at hand.

The third point I would like to mention very briefly, since it has been covered very thoroughly elsewhere in the book, is the need for every administrator to maximize his own effectiveness by realizing the full potential of his employees, particularly his key employees.

In any job plan that would bring out to the fullest the potential of all employees, the first step, of course, is to appraise their abilities, to know their strengths and weaknesses, to assign them jobs that will take advantage of their strengths and help overcome their weaknesses. Obviously job rotation plays an important part in this respect.

Another important element in maximizing the full potential of an employee is to minimize the great danger of his developing a do-nothing attitude fostered by a fear complex. A fear complex can easily arise from a demand for perfection when perfection is not required. Gradually the person reaches the point where he has been turned down so many times on decisions that he is fearful of acting, so he stops and makes no decisions at all. One thing we can surely agree on is that it is better to do something than nothing.

Lastly, I want again to mention, very briefly, the need for periodic self-appraisals of one's own effectiveness and the development of some set of standards against which to measure it. What these standards are is something each executive has to develop for himself, but let me suggest the following from my experience:

1. *A check on your specific contribution to the company's profit.* What is it you have particularly done that improves the company's profit or productivity — or whatever we wish to call the objective we are all constantly striving for — today, last week, last month, last year?

2. *A review of your accomplishment against a program of specific action.* The need for a written program of specific action cannot be overstated. I find it most helpful to have in writing a program for a definite period — a year or a month or even a day — as a yardstick for measuring my accomplishments.

3. *A constant check on the ability of your organization to operate without you.* No man is indispensable. The organization you head should be able to operate without you if you have been effective in your associations with it.

4. *A check on the willingness of others to join your organization.* It is good sometimes to question, "Do these people prefer us to others — or other people to us, other companies to ours, other supervisors to ours?"

Importance of Attitudes

The subject of this chapter smacks a little bit of "Ten Easy Lessons." So many books have been written on what to do, and I have seen so many people reading them. I know that when I read one of them, I say, "If I do this, and if I do that the way the book says, then I can get out of this staff job and be a big shot executive myself." Usually these "How To Do It" books come out of the hard experience of someone who has made a success, but the real secret of his success was the kind of man he was rather than the little techniques he used.

It seems to me that personal growth and increasing effectiveness are largely a matter of attitude rather than of techniques and skills. That is the one big point I want to make. The motives back of our efforts at self-improvement are probably much more important than the techniques which we learn.

I recall an incident at a conference when one of our officials was negotiating a deal with a pretty tough customer. It became clear that the customer was not putting all his cards on the table, and so he was told, "Excuse me, but your motives are showing." I think we sometimes fail in our efforts at self-improvement because our motives are showing. As a matter of fact, they always do. But we are likely to believe we are getting by without having them show.

Some of the slant I have on this subject comes from the practice in our company of making management appraisals. Three or four executives sit down together and discuss the performance of a subordinate about whom they know a good deal. Over the last seven years we have been appraising men in this way and I have been again and again impressed with the turn our discussions take.

As we appraise managers at lower levels in the organization, the analysis is likely to come out something like this: "Well, here's a good man. What he needs is more experience. Just give him a little time and knowledge. He needs to get this 'best man' training and he will be all right." Or, "He is all right. He's a good man, but he needs some more formal education. He ought to have some accounting." Or, "He should take the course in leadership." Or, "He knows his job, but he needs job rotation to broaden his base of experience." These are things the company might be doing for him, specific things. Or occasionally the conclusion may be, "This fellow is just too dumb and should be taken out of the management job."

As we move to higher levels in the organization, on the other hand, there is a pattern like this repeatedly: "Yes, this fellow is smart or he wouldn't be up this far in the organization. He is versatile. He's had the experience. He knows the business from A to Z. He's had the formal education; we even sent him to Harvard, you know." And the final judgment may be: "Yes, he has everything it takes to go up a notch higher in the management picture if it weren't for one little thing." And that one little thing is nearly always a matter of character or the man's sense of values. Call it what you will, there are certain intangibles in a man's sense of values, his attitude, his self-appraisal, which get communicated and affect his relationships with others.

Maybe we can be a little more specific. "O.K. he's fine. He has all kinds of ability, but you should see the way he handles his expense account. His expense account is terrible." "What is so wrong about that? Are you worrying about money?" "No, it isn't that, but the impression he creates on his subordinates. He wants to be a big shot; he is always grabbing the check. He is striving so hard to appear to be something which he is afraid he isn't." In other words, we just cannot see how this man can gain the respect or stature required in a higher executive position.

Or the executives sizing up a man may say: "Well, the only thing this fellow cares about is money. He is always asking for raises, and he's always thinking about money, large profits." I question whether that is the only criterion we should use, but that is not the point here. The point is that this is a man who is scheming and trying to get ahead and playing the game smart, but all the people he works with know his values are not sound, know he is selfish.

So I have become convinced that our effectiveness is a function of our motives, that what is in the heart is much more important than the techniques we use.

Let me put it another way. We have a number of units of operation that are essentially alike: sales units, sales districts, manufacturing plants, and so on. These operations, being in the same company, have the same wage policy, the same pension plans, the same benefit plans, the same kind of working conditions, the same kind of equipment. They have the same kind of trucks and the same kind of machines. They have the same staff help, the same personnel programs. They all have merit rating and job evaluation and the rest of the techniques and gadgets thrown at them.

Yet, year after year, we will have one unit where morale is

high, productivity is high, and everybody is having fun; and we will have another unit where morale is low, where we will have more gripes, and production is low. I investigate the cause of these differences and the nearest I can come to putting my finger on it is that the principal factor is the character of the boss.

For example, the whole philosophy of one of the men revolved around money; to him money was the most important thing. His attitude was: "I want to make all the money I can. I assume everybody else is trying to do likewise. I am going to negotiate the smartest deal I can to make the most for myself and let everyone work out his own problem." There was no end of trouble in his operation. And, needless to say, he is no longer with us.

Let us look at the reverse side. I can give you case after case of executives in our company who violate all the administrative practices that are taught in courses and who do many things wrong about managing, yet their employees are determined they are not going to let their boss fail because they feel he is a decent man. Such a man may not talk about his principles; he is not likely to say, "Here's my philosophy." But his employees instinctively know his character, and they respond to it more than to anything else. They know that he is "solid" and that he believes in them.

In preparation for this assignment, I asked some of our able young executives what they considered the most important aspect of becoming more effective and getting ahead in the organization. The answer I got so frequently that I began to wonder about it was, "Pick a good boss." So I asked them, "What do you mean by a good boss?" And they usually answered like this: "One who is interested in developing people, willing to delegate responsibility, willing to let his subordinates make some mistakes and learn by doing." "One who knows the business and can coach." "One who stands back of his men." "A boss you can believe in." There, in essence, is the quality that they thought was most important.

Now, it seems to me that this is significant — and not so surprising after all, when you think about it. For the real core of management is duplicating oneself through people, and therefore the skill of management is the motivation of people. People respond more to values and ideals than we give them credit for; and if our values are shallow, administrative techniques will not cover them up.

Now, what does this add up to? In order for an executive to increase his administrative effectiveness I would suggest that he begin by asking himself some questions along these lines:

What are my own objectives? Down deep in my heart what are the things I am striving for? What do I really want to accomplish? What do I want to do with my employees? What do I secretly want them to think of me? Do I really want to improve my administrative effectiveness and, if so, for what purpose? To get promoted? To get a raise? Is that something my employees are going to wave the flag about and say, "Let's help this fellow?"

Am I willing to pay the price? Are my desires single in purpose or contradictory? Do I have some barnacles of motivation that I still want to cling to as I try to progress even though they are a little bit contradictory, because I think I can get by with a few of them? (Did anybody in history ever make a real name for himself who wasn't devoted to a single objective? Did anybody ever make the grade on a half-hearted basis?)

I would also ask these questions: Do I set sound values for myself and my associates? Do I have a clear concept of the function of my business? (That is fundamental.) Do I define the functions and values of my unit in broad enough terms, in terms that will challenge me and my own employees? If we say the purpose of our business is to make money, should we be surprised if the employees down in the office say, "My purpose is to make more and more for myself, and I am going to join a union and make as much as I can."

We have held up, I think, ideals of self-acquisition, which do not bring out the best in people. In this area I would ask these questions: Do I really test the possibilities for creativity in individuals who work with me? Do I want to solve all the problems in order to show how good I am, or am I willing to let my subordinates have some of the fun? Am I also oriented downward, rather than only upward?

That kind of orientation demands some profound listening; we cannot assume we know the motives and attitudes of those whom we supervise. Usually, when we try so hard to find answers to problems, we get our blinders on and our vision is narrowed. We don't achieve results that are creative when our frame of mind is tense and when we try to force our own conclusions. It is natural to want to arrive at quick solutions, but the only safe approach demands a great deal of humility, patience, and effort to understand. There is a wisdom underlying life which we cannot sense and utilize if we do not listen profoundly and respectfully.

Of course, we have to recognize the realistic nature of competition. On the other hand, perhaps the competitive system, as we usually define it and as we usually try to sell it to our employees and to the American public generally, is of somewhat questionable value.

Does the competitive system make an enemy of those engaged in operations similar to ours; is our purpose to put our competitors out of business? Or is it our understanding of competition that we are trying to do the best possible job for the customer, that we have an obligation to him to become just as skillful and productive as possible? On such a basis, it seems to me, our competitive system not only is more salable but also will produce better results.

As to the profits, it seems to me that Jervis Babb, President of Lever Brothers, put the thing in proper perspective when he said in effect that profits are the yardstick that tell us whether we are doing the kind of social job we should be doing.[1] Approximately three-quarters of the population live in industry. Their satisfactions of life come out of their jobs. Therefore, industry has a great obligation to see that this life-on-the-job is something that is full and has some meaning. We must recognize that these people have certain ambitions. If we recognize this fact, our employees will become good producers and consequently we will make more money.

I have usually heard this sequence in the reverse order. The purpose of a business is to make money; the way to make money is to have high productivity and morale; the way to have high productivity and morale is to give these people some of the satisfactions they are looking for (usually with the qualification that the fringe benefits should be kept at a minimum). It should be the other way around. In terms of motivating people, there is a world of difference.

[1] Edward C. Bursk, Editor, *Getting Things Done in Business* (Cambridge, Harvard University Press, 1953), pp. 5–6.

To me it is very interesting to read the philosophies of some of our big companies. The Ford Motor Company, for instance, was not set up in business with any shallow idea of Henry Ford's to make as much money for himself as he could. As I understand it, it was his burning ambition to make transportation available to a great many people. And so you can go on from company to company; the great companies that have been in business and stayed in business are the ones that have developed high ideals and noble purposes to which people could dedicate themselves.

In summing up, I believe we should not try so hard to run the world but let others also have the satisfaction of exercising their talents. But most important of all, I think the values we adopt for ourselves will in the long run determine our effectiveness as executives more than will techniques and administrative practices.

Conclusion

Two different points of view on the subject of increasing our own administrative effectiveness have been presented in the preceding sections — one emphasizing techniques, the other emphasizing attitude and motivation. We had better not choose between them; we had better put them together if we can.

I am particularly interested in this subject from the point of view of when and how to take action. Actually, the energetic application of the kind of techniques just discussed, no matter how good, can lead to a distortion of the purposes underlying them — can lead not to conclusions and action but to delay and paralysis of motion — *if* people are not sharing the same energy, the same goals; *if* the men who apply these techniques are called upon to produce in an organization where morale is not high.

At the same time, no matter how good the attitude, lack of skillful techniques can equally well produce a kind of paralysis or delay resulting from good feeling, in which unpleasant things are postponed, in which the climate is ripe but nothing seems to happen, in which everybody is friendly but nobody starts.

The question is: How can we bring together the techniques and the attitudes so that leadership is exercised in a proper climate toward the attainment of *results?*

Somebody sometime has to take the initiative in deciding that this is the time to move. And the time schedule — for minimizing individuals' avoidance of problems and getting things done *and* for exercising sound values (on which motivation depends) — is not the same schedule as one based on getting the necessary information or doing the necessary preparation. Sometimes it is necessary to do something, to move in some direction, a little sooner than might be desirable if we were able to give exclusive attention to the questions of attitude.

I remember one committee meeting I attended. We were dealing with what seemed to us a complex problem. Finally, after several hours of discussion somebody settled back and said, "Well, the solution to this problem will emerge." That is a handy philosophy for such situations. But this time the chairman, who had some responsibility for getting results, looked up to say, "Who is going to emerge it?"

Somehow we must, in the scheme of things we have been discussing, make room for the exercise of some kind of technique and some kind of motivation to produce actual results — in terms of action and according to a time schedule, not of human aspirations and development, not of someone's personal desires, but in accordance with the exigencies of the market place.

When and how to take action are the crucial questions. When are people ready to move? When does the balance between competition and readiness of action on the part of the people with whom we have to work call for action? And then, how do we decide to do it?

I have only one simple technique to suggest as a supplement to those already discussed: that we start off with "Who else is involved?" and add to the list of jobs to be done the names of the people who will be affected by whatever decision is made and who are to be informed of whatever action is taken.

Certainly the integration of this matter of techniques and this matter of attitude depends on ability to perceive problems, and also to perceive where problems cut across various functions of an organization and impinge upon activities of people other than those in our own small bailiwick. We need to form the complete "jurisdiction" over a problem that will bring in the attitudes and contributions of other people whom it affects.

We have to take a kind of approach which exercises both an administrative skill and an attitude which extends beyond the particular job to which each of us is assigned. There really is no problem of choosing between techniques and attitudes, or ruling out one in favor of the other, if somehow we are able to get close to the thought that I am trying to express.

I suppose the objective, eventually, is to create in ourselves, and certainly to try to communicate to people with whom we work, the necessity for "the general management point of view."

This is a concept requiring abandonment of the fractional point of view and the integration of divisive and divided points of view, of pulling together specific, how-to-do-it techniques, according to their relative importance and our over-all basic values.

* * *

The administrative effectiveness of many executives depends upon their ability to release the creative talent of others under their control and direction. This involves the creation of a healthy climate in which to work. Subordinates should have freedom to make mistakes, but they should be expected to learn from them. The boss must expect to express the views of his organizational group in interdepartmental discussions, but he also has an obligation to give subordinates perspective on the needs of the company as a whole. He can increase effectiveness generally by providing good guidance when giving work assignments.

The executive can find time for what he ought to do by delegating some of his responsibilities to subordinates. It is a happy fact that delegation of work fits with the desire of many subordinates to assume more responsibility and show their abilities. Giving other men a chance speeds the process of executive development.

The delegating executive will increase his own and his subordinates' effectiveness by observing a few fundamentals. The responsibility of subordinates for action or recommendations should be defined. They should be held to producing the general-management type of solutions to problems. They should draw to the problem definition or the problem solution all the technical and intellectual resources of the company in whatever department they may be found. In the event of personal or departmental differences of opinion, the subordinate leader should resolve these differences and expedite action when it is imperative. Men should not be caught in what is a common fallacy: that the only test of coöperative action or good staff work is unanimous agreement. Some organizations are stultified by the equivalent of the UN veto.

Finally, the words "objective," "conception," and "perception" can have real meaning for the effective executive. A company will not accomplish its economic and social responsibilities unless the majority of its people have common perceptions of the goals of the company and the parts they play. They must be able to conceive the multitude of personal and technical relationships that produce a live, profitable company. The executive who helps other men widen their perceptions will not have to rely on detailed directives to accomplish action. He will be producing subordinates who know what to do and have capacity to handle tough problems. He will be building an organization that can take the intelligent type of action implicit throughout our discussion. Furthermore this executive will be a leader who has satisfied followers; his motives will be clear, and they will pass muster.

SUPPLEMENT
HOW TO INCREASE EXECUTIVE EFFECTIVENESS
A SELECTED BIBLIOGRAPHY

A SELECTED BIBLIOGRAPHY

Prepared for the Twenty-Third National Business Conference of the Harvard Business School Association, June 13, 1953 by Mrs. Harriette L. Williams of the Reference Department, Baker Library, Harvard Graduate School of Business Administration.

The books in the first section deal with administration and management for the most part, but not exclusively, in the field of business. They have been selected because of their authors' original thinking, or stimulating and thought-provoking exposition of significant ideas. The sections which follow deal with more specific subjects. Although the principles discussed apply to all levels of management, the emphasis is on top management and no works dealing primarily with supervisors have been included. The list is selective rather than comprehensive, with bibliographies listed that provide material for more exhaustive study.

Administration and Management

Barnard, Chester I., *The Functions of the Executive* (Cambridge: Harvard University Press, 1938). 334 pp.

"Still the classic application to the task of management of the conceptual approach called Human Relations and by all odds the most profound and original book on achieving coöperation in business organizations written by a practicing executive." — Kenneth R. Andrews "Looking Around," *Harvard Business Review,* XXVIII, No. 2 (March 1950), pp. 147–161.

Barnard, Chester I., *Organization and Management; Selected Papers* (Cambridge: Harvard University Press, 1938). 244 pp.

Includes papers on the nature of leadership and leadership in the democratic process, concepts of organization, personnel relations, education for executives, status systems in formal organization.

Follett, Mary Parker, *Dynamic Administration; the Collected Papers of Mary Parker Follett,* edited by Henry C. Metcalf and L. Urwick (N. Y.: Harper & Brothers [1941]). 320 pp.

Includes papers on constructive conflict, giving of orders, business as an integrative unity, power, responsibility in business management, psychology of control, psychology of consent and participation, leadership theory and practice.

Gulick, Luther, and L. Urwick, eds., *Papers on the Science of Administration* (N. Y.: Columbia University, Institute of Public Administration, 1937). 195 pp.

Essays by James D. Mooney, Henri Fayol, Henry S. Dennison, L. J. Henderson, Mary Parker Follett, John Lee, V. A. Graicunas, and the editors.

Merrill, Harwood F., ed., *The Responsibilities of Business Leadership* (Cambridge: Harvard University Press, 1948). 93 pp.

Papers on responsibilities of businessmen to the public, employees, government, consumers, stockholders and the world, based on speeches made at the Eighteenth Annual Conference of the Harvard Business School Association, June 12, 1948, with an introduction by Dean Donald Kirk David.

Mooney, James D., and Alan C. Reiley, *The Principles of Organization* (N. Y., Harper & Brothers, 1939). 223 pp.

Principles of organization with illustrations from constitutional government, the Roman Catholic Church, military and industrial organization.

Roethlisberger, F. J., *Management and Morale* (Cambridge, Harvard University Press, 1947). 194 pp.

The author uses illustrations from research in industrial plants to show that effective human control can be exercised by a person in a position of responsibility only through an adequate understanding of the human situations he is administering.

Simon, Herbert A., *Administrative Behavior; a Study of Decision-Making Processes in Administrative Organization* (N. Y.: The Macmillan Company, 1947). 259 pp.

A study of "organization, the administrative process, the nature of decision and elements of value and fact entering into decisions." — Preface.

Tead, Ordway, *The Art of Administration* (N. Y.: McGraw-Hill Book Company, Inc., 1951). 223 pp.

"Here . . . are reliable analyses of basic human forces, clear-cut statements of administrative responsibilities, sound management philosophy, plus suggestions on how to increase executives' competence and skill." — Foreword by Lawrence A. Appley.

Urwick, L., *The Elements of Administration* (N. Y.: Harper & Brothers [1943]). 132 pp.

Based on five lectures presenting in a "coherent and logical pattern the principles of organization formulated by different authorities."

Whitehead, T. N., *Leadership in a Free Society; a Study in Human Relations Based on an Analysis of Present-Day Industrial Civilization* (Cambridge: Harvard University Press, 1936). 266 pp.

"A free society must be an integrated, responsible society, capable of adjusting intelligently to its own changing situation. This book attempts to point the way to suitable techniques of observation and interpretation by which we may gain the knowledge that we lack today." — Preface.

Bibliography

Hopf, Harry A., *Soundings in the Literature of Management; Fifty Books the Educated Practitioner Should Know* (Ossining, N. Y.: Hopf Institute of Management, 1945). (Publication No. 6.) Reprinted in Sources of Business Information by Edwin T. Coman, Jr., pp. 156–177. (N. Y.: Prentice-Hall, Inc., 1949.)

An annotated bibliography of books which this authority on the literature of management considers basic.

A Reading List on Business Administration (Hanover, N. H.: Dartmouth College, The Amos Tuck School of Business Administration, sixth revision, May 1, 1952). 68 pp.

A selected, annotated reading list prepared by the Faculty of The Amos Tuck School of Business Administration.

Planning the Organization Structure

American Management Association, *Organization Controls and Executive Compensation* (N. Y., 1948). General Management Series, No. 142.

"Organization Controls in Industry," by General Brehon Somervell, pp. 3–13; "Organization as the Mechanism of Management," by Lounsbury Fish, pp. 14–26.

American Management Association, *Organization Planning and Management Development* (N. Y., 1951). Personnel Series, No. 141.

"Dynamics and Mechanics of Organization" by Ernest Dale, pp. 3–14, discusses major management complaints against prevalent ideas and practice; "Organization Planning — Its Challenges and Limitations" by Charles R. Hook, Jr., pp. 15–22, outlines reasons for failure of organization plans.

Cordiner, Ralph J., "Problems of Management in a Large Decentralized Organization" [General Electric Company], pp. 3–17 in Developing

Management Leadership for a Free Society (N. Y.: American Management Association, 1952). General Management Series, No. 159.

Dale, Ernest, *Planning and Developing the Company Organization Structure* (N. Y.: American Management Association, 1952). 232 pp. Research Report No. 20.

Part I of this report of a two-year study analyzes major organizational problems at various stages of a company's growth. Part II deals with the mechanics of organization. Appendices include data on top management job descriptions, committees, extent of decentralization, major management functions.

Holden, Paul E., Lounsbury S. Fish and Hubert L. Smith, *Top Management Organization and Control; a Research Study of the Management Policies and Practices of Thirty-One Leading Industrial Corporations,* enl. ed. (N. Y.: McGraw-Hill Book Company, Inc., Published for the Stanford University Graduate School of Business, 1951). 257 pp.

Part B "Organization Practices," pp. 15–103, covers top management, operating, staff, and committee organization with illustrative charts.

National Industrial Conference Board, *Organization Standards and Practices by Thomas A. Fitzgerald* (N. Y., 1946). 33 pp. Studies in Business Policy No. 18.

Concise review of the principles of organization; comparisons with prevailing practices as indicated by organization charts.

Newman, William H., *Administrative Action: The Techniques of Organization and Management* (N. Y.: Prentice-Hall, Inc., 1951). 483 pp.

Exposition of "basic processes of administration: planning, organizing, assembling resources, directing, controlling." Comprehensive, readable discussion of principles of organization and organization structure in Part II, "Organizing," pp. 123–303.

Petersen, Elmore, and E. Grosvenor Plowman, *Business Organization and Management,* rev. ed. (Homewood, Ill.: Richard D. Irwin, Inc., 1949).

A text with useful chapters on departmental structure, line, staff, and functional organization, and centralization and decentralization, chaps. VIII–XII, pp. 200–308.

Standard Oil Company of California. Department on Organization, *The Management Guide; the Development of the Management Guide as an Organization and Administrative Aid by George Lawrence Hall* [San Francisco] 1948. 74 pp.

Discussion of the purpose of a management guide, its essential elements, preparation and use. Management guides for a hypothetical business based on the theory and practice, but not reflecting actual positions in the Standard Oil Company of California, are used as illustrations.

Bibliography

Dale, Ernest, *Planning and Developing the Company Organization Structure* (N. Y.: American Management Association, 1952). Research Report No. 20. "Bibliography," pp. 213–225.

WORK OF THE EXECUTIVE

American Management Association, *The Chief Executive's Job Today, a Reappraisal* (N. Y.: 1952). 42 pp. General Management Series, No. 155.

Includes the title article by James B. Du Paru and Presidents' Round Table discussions of "Organization of the President's Job" and "The President's Current Operating Problems."

Baker, John Calhoun, *Directors and Their Functions, a Preliminary Study* (Boston: Harvard University, Graduate School of Business Administration, Division of Research, 1945). 145 pp.

First publication resulting from a study of management problems of large industrial corporations and the relationship of directors to these problems. Chaps. IV–VII are case studies of four companies.

Copeland, Melvin T., and Andrew R. Towl, *The Board of Directors and Business Management* (Boston: Harvard University, Graduate School of Business Administration, Division of Research, 1947). 202 pp.

A study of the relations of directors, both as individuals and as a group, to business management, with many examples of actual situations. There are chapters on selection of executives, policy-making, checking up on results, incentives for directors, selection of directors.

Copeland, Melvin T., *The Executive at Work* (Cambridge: Harvard University Press, 1951). 278 pp.

Discusses the elements of executive achievement with reference primarily to corporate business enterprises, but many of the conclusions apply to executive leadership in nonbusiness enterprises.

Dimock, Marshall E., *The Executive in Action* (N. Y.: Harper & Brothers, 1945). 276 pp.

A discussion of executive functions and techniques based on the author's experience, largely in government agencies. Analyzes management problems in starting a new enterprise using as an example the Recruitment and Management Organization of the War Shipping Administration.

Gordon, Robert Aaron, *Business Leadership in the Large Corporation* (Washington, The Brookings Institution, 1945). 369 pp.

A study of corporate practice to determine who performs the functions of business leadership and under what conditions; the role of the executive board, the stockholders, influence of financial and other interest groups, the role of government.

Holden, Paul E., Lounsbury S. Fish and Hubert L. Smith, *Top Management Organization and Control; a Research Study of the Management Policies and Practices of Thirty-One Leading Industrial Corporations,* enl. ed. (N. Y.: McGraw-Hill Book Company, Inc., Published for the Stanford University Graduate School of Business, 1951). 257 pp.

Part C, "Control Practices," pp. 77–210, covers control in principal management fields, policy, organization, operation, personnel, finance, research and development, public relations.

Learned, Edmund P., David N. Ulrich and Donald R. Booz, *Executive Action* (Boston: Harvard University, Graduate School of Business Administration, Division of Research, 1951). 218 pp.

A study of the human aspects of executives' problems in securing effective coöperation. Based on intensive investigation of working relationships among executives in twelve companies, the "cases" used at the Harvard Business School and the experience of Faculty and research staff.

Mace, Myles L., *The Board of Directors in Small Corporations* (Boston: Harvard University, Graduate School of Business Administration, Division of Research, 1948). 92 pp.

The author concludes from the situations encountered in the study that "active, able, and continuously interested members of small corporation boards of directors can serve as useful sources of management assistance." Examples from actual company experiences show how directors can assist the manager.

Niles, Mary Cushing Howard, *Middle Management; the Job of the Junior Administrator,* rev. ed. (N. Y.: Harper & Brothers, 1949). 274 pp.

Problems of the intermediate officers [between top management and supervisors] who deal with all the other levels of rank and responsibility.

Executive Development

Andrews, Kenneth R., "Executive Training by the Case Method," pp. 193–212 in *The Case Method of Teaching Human Relations and*

Administration, an Interim Statement, edited by Kenneth R. Andrews (Cambridge: Harvard University Press, 1953). Reprinted from *Harvard Business Review,* XXIX, No. 5 (Sept. 1951), pp. 58–70.

Essentials for success in training in the human aspects of administration by the case method; with examples from the experience of Cargill, Inc. and the American Red Cross.

Bower, Marvin, ed., *The Development of Executive Leadership* (Cambridge: Harvard University Press, 1949). 130 pp.

Based on speeches at the Nineteenth Annual Conference of the Harvard Business School Association, June 11, 1949. Part I: "The Kind of Business Leaders We Need"; Part II: "Steps in Developing the Kind of Business Leaders We Need."

Bradshaw, T. F., *Developing Men for Controllership* (Boston: Harvard University, Graduate School of Business Administration, Division of Research, 1950). 231 pp.

A study of management personnel development methods of those companies in which the controller has already stepped out of his accounting specialty and into a larger management role.

Dooher, M. Joseph, and Vivienne Marquis, eds., *The Development of Executive Talent: a Handbook of Management Development Techniques and Case Studies* (N. Y.: American Management Association, 1952). 576 pp.

Articles from *Personnel,* papers presented at AMA conferences, supplemented by many especially prepared chapters integrated into a practical manual. Includes case studies of the programs in 17 companies.

Given, William B., *Bottom-Up Management* (N. Y.: Harper & Brothers, 1949). 171 pp.

Discusses the ways in which American Brake Shoe Company passes authority down the line, encourages the lower ranks to try out their own ideas, gives each person the greatest possible opportunity for self-development.

In *Reaching Out in Management* (Harper & Brothers, 1953) the author develops further his philosophy of management.

Habbe, Stephen, *Company Programs of Executive Development* (N. Y.: National Industrial Conference Board, 1950). 64 pp. Studies in Personnel Policy No. 107.

A chapter on the over-all picture and nine case studies of company programs.

McCormick, Charles P., *The Power of People: Multiple Management Up to Date* (N. Y.: Harper & Brothers, 1949). 136 pp.

McCormick & Company's experience with executive development

through participation in four management boards. His earlier book on the plan is *Multiple Management* (Harper & Brothers, 1938).

Mace, Myles L., *The Growth and Development of Executives* (Boston, Harvard University, Graduate School of Business Administration, Division of Research, 1950). 200 pp.

Examination of the policies, formal programs, and practices of manufacturing companies for developing men for responsible management positions. Twenty-five companies were studied in detail.

McGregor, Douglas M., *Getting Effective Leadership in the Industrial Organization* (Cambridge: Massachusetts Institute of Technology, Dept. of Economics and Social Science). 5 pp. Publications in Social Science, Series 2, No. 16, 1944. Appeared in *Journal of Consulting Psychology,* VIII, No. 2 (March–April 1944), pp. 55–63 and *Advanced Management,* IX, No. 4 (Oct.–Dec. 1944), pp. 148–153.

Conditions under which the subordinate, at any level of the industrial organization, can realize his own potentialities.

Riegel, John W., *Executive Development: a Survey of Experience in Fifty American Corporations* (Ann Arbor: University of Michigan Press, 1952). 369 pp. Bureau of Industrial Relations, Report No. 5.

This report outlines a comprehensive program of executive development, its underlying philosophy and methods of accomplishment, based on the experience and views of the companies studied. Chapter XX, "University Programs for Executives," pp. 309–362, summarizes the types of programs offered, the advantages and weaknesses of each.

Selekman, Benjamin M., "Wanted Mature Managers," pp. 141–172 in his *Labor Relations and Human Relations* (N. Y.: McGraw-Hill Book Company, 1947). Reprinted from *Harvard Business Review,* XXIV, No. 2 (Winter 1946), pp. 228–244.

"Never before . . . have industrial leaders been in such need of emotional maturity." Normal individuals can develop the emotional and social maturity required. Training, both in university courses and on the job, is needed to develop insight into human behavior.

University Training for Executives

Carson, Waller, Jr., "Looking Around: Management Training," in *Harvard Business Review,* XXXI, No. 2 (March–April 1953), pp. 141–155.

Objectives of various university executive training courses, method used, and data on programs; suggested references, p. 155.

Education for Management; Report of a Visit to the U.S.A. in 1951 of a

British Specialist Team Concerned with Education for Management (London: Anglo-American Council on Productivity, 1951). 86 pp.

Information about management training in American universities and the Team's opinions based on their observations.

"M. I. Guide to Executive Schools," in *Modern Industry,* XXIV, No. 3 [Sept. 15, 1952], pp. 56–64.

Digest of information on college and university courses for business executives.

Smith, Dan Throop, "Education for Administration," in *Harvard Business Review,* XXIII, No. 3 (Spring 1945), pp. 360–371.

Discussion of the elements of good administration, which of them may be learned and in what way their teaching can be effective.

Teele, Stanley F., "The Business Schools and Executive Development." In *Advanced Management,* XVIII, No. 1 (Jan. 1953), pp. 25–28.

Ways in which the business schools can contribute to the development of executives.

Walker, Ross G., "A Lesson in Training Techniques," pp. 109–119 in *Getting Things Done in Business,* edited by Edward C. Bursk (Cambridge: Harvard University Press, 1953).

A talk by Professor Walker on the Harvard Business School's Advanced Management Program at the Twenty-Second National Business Conference sponsored by the Harvard Business School Association, June 7, 1952.

Bibliographies

Dooher, M. Joseph, and Vivienne Marquis, eds., *The Development of Executive Talent* (N. Y.: American Management Association, 1952). "Selected References," pp. 553–571.

Executive Development (Harvard University, Graduate School of Business Administration, Baker Library, April 1952). 10 pp. Supplement, May 1953. 5 pp. Reference List No. 11.

Books, pamphlets, and periodical articles, many of them on development programs of individual companies.

Executive Development. Business Information Sources. Bulletin of the Cleveland Public Library LII, No. 3 (July–Sept. 1952). 4 pp.

An annotated list which supplements the issue of June 1947, Leadership and Management and contains references published since that date.

Riegel, John W., *Executive Development* (Ann Arbor: University of Michigan Press, 1952). Bureau of Public Relations, Report, No. 5.

Appendix B, "Selected References on Executive Development," pp. 362–364.

FINANCIAL INCENTIVES FOR EXECUTIVES

Casey, William J., and J. K. Lasser, *Executive Pay Plans, 1952–1953* (N. Y.: Business Reports Inc., 1952). 160 pp.

"This study aims to help top management and its professional advisers to analyze company and executive requirements and to formulate [an executive pay] plan to meet those requirements." More than 100 company plans were analyzed and the most valuable features of the best plans are presented here. — Introduction.

Dartnell Corporation, *Compensation of Management Personnel* (Chicago, 1952).

A Dartnell survey in the form of ten loose-leaf reports which include discussion of compensation plans, statistical data on salary ranges by industry, and sample salary plans for general, financial, production and operating personnel and sales management and junior executives. In the report on chief executives there are tables of salaries paid in 49 large industrial corporations and 199 insurance companies.

Fetter, Robert B., and Donald C. Johnson, *Compensation and Incentives for Industrial Executives* (Bloomington, Ind.: Indiana University Press, 1952). 208 pp.

A study to determine "how able executives are to be compensated so that (1) they are induced to exert their most productive efforts, and (2) their rewards are economically and socially acceptable." Opinions of executives, labor leaders, and economists are quoted in answer to the second question. Summaries of the compensation plans of fifty large companies selected for study are given in the appendix.

Hall, Challis A., Jr., *Effects of Taxation; Executive Compensation and Retirement Plans* (Boston: Harvard University, Graduate School of Business Administration, Division of Research, 1951). 365 pp.

Examines the various forms of executive compensation to determine and explain their relative growth and present importance to corporations and executives, and to describe in detail their tax advantages to both. In later chapters he deals with effects on executives' mobility, performance, and retirement of specific forms of compensation and retirement plans.

Hopf, Harry Arthur, *Executive Compensation and Accomplishment* (N. Y.: American Management Association, 1945). 22 pp. Financial Management Series, No. 78.

Dr. Hopf discusses the objectives to be attained, elements and scope of the plan, underlying principles, measurement of accomplishment, and obstacles to successful administration.

Sanders, Thomas H., *Effects of Taxation on Executives* (Boston: Harvard University, Graduate School of Business Administration, Division of Research, 1951). 229 pp.

In a companion volume to Hall's *Executive Compensation,* Professor Sanders deals with attitudes of executives toward the general level of individual taxation and the effects on the executives' efforts, intensity and duration of their active business careers, their retirement, and their struggles to achieve personal financial competence. Based primarily on personal interviews.

Washington, George Thomas, and V. Henry Rothschild II, *Compensating the Corporate Executive,* rev. ed. (N. Y.: The Ronald Press, 1951). 586 pp.

A handbook for executives and their counsel on the economic and legal aspects of executive compensation. "Corporate Documents" in the appendix, pp. 425–563, include compensation contracts of all types.

Bibliographies

Executive Compensation: Selected References, 1947–1952 (Boston: Harvard University, Graduate School of Business Administration, Baker Library, May 1952). 7 pp. Reference List No. 13.

A list of books, pamphlets, and periodical articles which supplements Reference List No. 2, *Executive Compensation,* Dec. 1947.

Industrial Pensions, compiled by Guest W. Perry (Boston: Harvard University, Graduate School of Business Administration, Baker Library, May 1953). 13 pp. Reference List No. 14.

A selected list with some brief annotations.